"As a GB rowing coach, I have seen countless young rowers use willpower to overcome physical disadvantages and achieve success. This book promotes the benefits of willpower for everyone, while providing the tools you need to acquire it."

Iain Somerside, GB Rowing Coach

"I used to believe that willpower was in the genes; you either had it or you hadn't. This book has changed my mind and convinced me that willpower is a learnable skill."

Gordon Baker, CEO, JMT Consultants

Willpower

Willpower

Discover It,
Use It and Get
What You Want

Ros Taylor

CAPSTONE

This edition first published 2017

© 2017 Ros Taylor

Registered office
John Wiley & Sons Ltd, The Atrium, Southern Gate, Chichester, West Sussex, PO19 8SQ, United Kingdom

For details of our global editorial offices, for customer services and for information about how to apply for permission to reuse the copyright material in this book please see our website at www .wiley.com.

Wiley publishes in a variety of print and electronic formats and by print-on-demand. Some material included with standard print versions of this book may not be included in e-books or in print-on-demand. If this book refers to media such as a CD or DVD that is not included in the version you purchased, you may download this material at http://booksupport.wiley.com. For more information about Wiley products, visit www.wiley.com.

Library of Congress Cataloging-in-Publication Data is available

A catalogue record for this book is available from the British Library.

ISBN 978-0-857-08719-5 (pbk) ISBN 978-0-857-08714-0 (ebk)
ISBN 978-0-857-08721-8 (ebk)

Cover Design: Wiley

10 9 8 7 6 5 4 3 2 1

Set in 11/13 Myriad Pro Light by Aptara Inc., New Delhi, India

Printed in Great Britain by TJ International Ltd, Padstow, Cornwall, UK

Contents

Preface   ix
    Questionnaires   x
    The Stories   x
    Your Willpower Challenge   xi
    What's Inside   xii
    Final Thoughts   xiv

PART ONE – THE ESSENCE OF WILLPOWER   **1**
    Willpower Ingredients in Abby's Story   3
    Directions for Completing the Willpower Scale   4
    The Willpower Scale   5
    Willpower Research   8
    Willpower is a Game of Two Brains   11
    Willpower is a Limited Resource . . . or is it?   17
    New Research to Challenge Willpower as a Limited Resource 19
    Mark Masson on Willpower and Health   21

PART TWO – GOALS AND VISION   **23**
    Why Goals?   23
    Goal Planning   28
    Your Willpower Goals   30
    How You Learn   34
    Motivation   43
    A Theory of Motivation   44
    Remember Your Goals   46
    Inspiring You Toward Your Willpower Challenge   51

PART THREE – NEW HABITS FOR OLD   **55**
    Origins of Willpower with Graham Allen   57
    Ego States   60
    The Willpower Stage of Habit Formation   62
    The Extinction Burst   64
    Mini and Multiple Habits   68
    Alternatively, Start Big   71
    Becoming Failure Proof   72
    Elite Performers and 10 000 Hours of Repetition   74
    Good Habits Made Easy   77

PART FOUR – THE WILLPOWER MINDSET   **87**
    So How Can We All Acquire a Murray Mindset?   88
    Reality Thinking   101
    Externalise Your Thinking   103
    Useful Thinking   104
    Achieve a Willpower Mindset   105

PART FIVE – WILLPOWER AND WORK   **113**
    Self-Awareness   115
    Skills for Business Success   120
    Create: The Process for Organisational Change   137
    Pilot   140
    Launch   140
    Coach   141
    Evaluate   141
    The Willpower of Your Own Business   142
    How to Stick to Your Willpower Challenge at Work   152

FINAL THOUGHTS   **155**
    Highlights   156

Acknowledgements   *157*
About the Author   *159*

Preface

Willpower is a series of recipes for willpower success seasoned with some inspirational case studies from adventurers, athletes, Paralympians, CEOs, teenagers and those who have struggled with addiction and adversity. *Willpower* is dissected and served up in bite-sized pieces so that you can use these tips in your own life for immediate effect.

Willpower is for everyone who wants to be successful in life and work: the unemployed person who wants a job, the graduate setting out on their career, the woman returner, the writer of their first book, the manager desiring to become a leader, the leader wanting to get to the board, the parent wanting to teach willpower to their children, the coach encouraging willpower in their clients

If you think willpower is a Victorian out-of-date concept, think again. Researchers have found that willpower is a better predictor of life and work success than IQ. Children with low willpower are four times more likely to have low-paying jobs, be overweight, have drug and alcohol problems, have short-rather than long-term relationships and have a criminal conviction.

So willpower is the very heartbeat of a successful, engaged and fulfilling life, and is not down to an accident of birth but a series of skills you can put into practice immediately with the help of this practical book.

This book is based on techniques that are known to work, so simply choose which relate to you and put them into practice. There is a three-week rule:

try a new skill every day for three weeks and repeat for nine to turn it into a habit.

This book is self-help for self-control.

QUESTIONNAIRES

I have included in each part of the book a number of questionnaires and checklists to gauge how much willpower you have, how you utilise goals, whether you are an optimist or pessimist, or even knowing if you could have the willpower to become an entrepreneur.

Where some established measures have been lengthy, I have shortened them. There is nothing worse than wading through 370 questions when you get the same result with a dozen. Where there is nothing on the market, I have conceived the questionnaires myself and tested them on my clients before you. No person was harmed in this endeavour.

My rationale for these tests is that I want you to become an expert in your own willpower: understanding your strengths and willpower glitches. With that knowledge, you will be that much more successful in negotiating the ups and downs of getting to where you want to be. Knowing when you generally give in to temptation gives you advance warning to initiate your "plan to fail plan".

THE STORIES

A major part of this book is the stories we collected from a diverse group of people selected for their willpower and remarkable achievements.

Judy Murray talks about her sons' willpower to become winners and her own to continue to coach women's tennis with few resources.

Jamie Andrew, quadruple amputee, tells us about returning to challenges like the London Marathon and climbing Kilimanjaro.

Phil Howard, Michelin star chef, discusses the pressures of the job, his drug addiction and how an exercise habit replaced his drug habit.

Neil Fachie, gold medal-winning Paralympian cyclist, tells about his preparations for the Rio Olympics.

Justine Roberts, founder and CEO of Mumsnet, talks about the delayed gratification of running your own business.

Julie Ashmore, business woman and mother of two, shares her adventuring stories of going to both North and South Poles.

Gordon Baker, CEO of JMT Consultants, discusses the limitations of willpower at work and what you need to be successful. His son Jamie also recounts his story about the power of visualisation.

Sir Richard Greenbury, former Chairman and CEO of Marks and Spencer, advises what will help you get to the top of an organisation.

Julian Richer, CEO of Richer Sounds, really grasps the nature of motivation at work and shares his methods.

Dame Stella Rimington, former Director General of MI5, discusses confidence and its place in getting to the top.

Charlie Mullins, plumber extraordinaire, shares his joy in owning his own business and the willpower it takes to be successful.

Mark Masson, specialist recruiter, recounts his fight with cancer and the part willpower played in his recovery.

Todd Whiteford, who had testicular cancer but decided to run in the Marathon des Sables between his surgery and chemotherapy, provides us with the story and the outcome.

Abby, a social phobic who had to be schooled at home, tells us what prised her from the house and how willpower helped her get her life back.

Grace Boyle, an alcoholic, describes how the help of Alcoholics Anonymous and willpower brought her back from the brink.

Iain Somerside, GB rowing coach, talks about the willpower mindset which creates Olympian winners.

Turly Humphrey, founder and CEO of Circle Sports, talks about her organisation which helps unemployed young people achieve jobs.

Graham Allen, Member of Parliament for Nottingham North, tells us about his work on the "Early Years" project and the difference interventions can make to generations of lives.

YOUR WILLPOWER CHALLENGE

I would like you to take the opportunity to pursue a Willpower Challenge or indeed Challenges of your own as you read the book. Your Challenge may be:

- A *dream* you might have had for some time but may have lacked confidence or time to pursue. It might be skydiving, parachute jumping, adventuring to unusual places or going to university or college to pursue further education.

- Something *meaningful* in your life, like raising money for a charitable cause, a test of endurance or "staying alive" – as one of our willpower interviewees admitted as he coped with a terminal disease.
- A *habit you want to break* – smoking, alcohol, drugs or overeating. You may have tried before to overcome a behaviour and even been partially successful, then returned to your old ways. Make this the time to be successful for all time.
- A *habit you want to establish* – for example, healthy eating, an exercise regime, a better sleep pattern, a calmer demeanour, an interest in people around you.
- A *desire to win* in a sport of your choice, perhaps to Olympic standard or for social and personal enjoyment. We certainly meet a plethora of impressive sports personalities and coaches in succeeding pages.
- *Promotion at work* demands willpower and a variety of skills. Learn the leadership skills suggested by top CEOs and start to become more successful at work.
- *Start your own business*. Discover if you have the willpower necessary to be an entrepreneur and hear from others who have made that leap and their journey to success.

WHAT'S INSIDE

Part One: The Essence of Willpower

This title sounds a bit like a scent – but willpower can't be sprayed on, inhaled or handed to someone else to do it for you. It is you in charge of you.

Part One reviews willpower research and comes to the conclusion that the "muscle" analogy, much utilised by researchers and psychologists in the past, does not fit with recent experiments. So I re-examine the latest thinking to help you achieve willpower.

There are inspirational stories from a young girl who had been confined to her house for four years before emerging using amazing willpower, amputees who are back adventuring, the ill or damaged who have willed themselves back to life. If they can do that, what could you do?

So, the essence of willpower is about how you harness your self-control to get where you want to go, and this part of the book helps you start to understand how to do that.

Part Two: Goals and Vision
Goals and Vision will help you address your own Willpower Challenges, working out what is meaningful for you to achieve, turning your dreams into goals. How you do that with goal planning, as well as how you implement these goals, is assessed and discussed.

Working on the steps to your goals and visualising them have been shown to increase positive outcomes, so there are some great stories around the power of visualisation with instructions for you to gain the same outcomes.

How you like to learn should guide you in choosing the "how" of pursuing your goals: should that be in a group with others, by reading and understanding, by practical steps or by experimentation? Understanding your learning preferences increases the likelihood of willpower success.

Part Three: New Habits for Old
At least 50% of what we do is down to habit. And our habits are established early on in our lives, copied from our parents or parent substitutes. If that knowledge fills you with dread, as the way your parents behaved is not how you want to be, help is at hand. I outline how habits are established and how bad ones can be changed and replaced with better versions. The purpose of willpower is a drive towards useful habits so that you achieve long-term success with your Willpower Challenge.

If you want to become the best in class for a skill, there is advice on how to achieve that as well as establishing some generic good habits that will prolong your life on earth.

When things go belly up with your own Willpower Challenges, because life is rarely plain sailing, we discuss how you can get over a glitch and move on instead of indulging in self-castigation.

Part Four: The Willpower Mindset
Willpower is a mindset and gaining that mindset is important to get those willpower ducks in a row. If you tell yourself it will never work then … it won't.

Just knowing about a willpower mindset doesn't, of course, mean you will have one. It takes a bit of work to achieve, so this part of the book explores how to achieve a relentlessly positive mindset. You can't leap from negative to positive thinking overnight. That would be the stuff of delusion. There are easy steps presented here that will progress your thinking: understanding your negative thoughts and where they come from, exploring the evidence for their existence, trying out useful thinking before finally achieving a positive willpower mindset.

Learn here about the power of externalisation to remain cool in a crisis, how to have a growth mindset and achieve the same mental strength of winners like Wimbledon tennis players and Olympic rowers. All to help with your Willpower Challenge.

Part Five: Willpower and Work

If your Willpower Challenge is about success at work and getting to the top, then focus on Part Five of the book.

Willpower at Work is not just about you but the motivation of others around you, so Part Five presents the three S's of Willpower at work: Self-Awareness, Skills and Self-Preservation.

You get the chance to complete the Willpower at Work scale to rate your abilities before plugging the gaps with the skills suggested. I interviewed 80 CEOs and asked them to rate what made them successful so others could follow in their footsteps. Six of the skills they suggested are outlined here with tips on how to achieve mastery.

We hear from corporate greats as well as entrepreneurs about their views about willpower and how they came to be top of their game.

Stress at work is prevalent nowadays, with more demands and fewer resources, but a job shouldn't shorten your existence. Strategies to be fit for the fray are proposed so you will be around for many more Willpower Challenges.

FINAL THOUGHTS

I would love you to share your Willpower Challenges with me, warts and all: what worked for you and what was less successful. Your stories will help others face their dreams, goals, desires – and perhaps demons.

Share your willpower stories on my website (www.rostaylorcompany .com), Twitter (@Ros_Taylor_Co), and Facebook (www.facebook.com/ RosTaylorCompany).

PART ONE

The Essence of Willpower

Abby became a volunteer at Canal College, which is part of the Scottish Waterways Trust and helps young people like Abby acquire job experience to go on to further education or employment. Canal College also helps the environment by improving British canals and the surrounding areas. I'll let her tell you her story.

> "I'd left school in my second year to be home schooled. A mixture of health problems and anxiety had led me to be unable to cope in school anymore. I still finished all my exams and stuff, completed my education, just not in school. So because of that I wasn't socialising. I had almost three years of no socialising with people my own age. And that led to my anxiety getting worse. I never went out, never had any friends, so I became the ultimate recluse. I just could not talk to people. The only person I spoke to was my mum, that was it, I didn't have anyone else.
>
> Well once I'd finished with the home schooling, Canal College was suggested to me because I like nature and it was outdoors. At first I refused. I'm not doing that, no chance, no! I will admit just the thought of it gave me a few panic attacks, but I eventually I said, yeah ok, I'll sign up for that, but I won't get the placement. And then it turned out I did get the placement and then oh no, I don't want to do this. I went to the interview and although I was very quiet, they were willing to give me a chance, so I took it and I went and it was terrifying.

I felt a mixture of fear and excitement. I was happy that I'd got something and I was determined to get over my anxiety. I was working through it, but I was also really nervous about how I'd cope because I hadn't ever been in a group of people my age. So it was a huge step.

Just having to look someone in the eye was a big thing for me. I couldn't talk to people. I remember when I first got to college. It was the first day; I just sat in the corner and didn't talk to anyone. The only people who tried to talk to me were the mentors, the adults who are there to try and help the young people.

Some nights I just couldn't sleep. Even though I was literally trembling, I forced myself to go, no matter how uncomfortable I felt. I never missed a day. There was one day where I was genuinely sick, but no matter how nervous I felt, I always made myself go. This was my chance, I kept telling myself.

During those first two or three weeks, people talked to me and I found that helpful because I definitely wasn't going to talk to them. But about three weeks in, I started talking back to the people who were trying to talk to me. I really didn't know how to interact with people, so sometimes I would sit and watch to see what they did, how people interacted with each other, to work out what was normal. Kind of looking for tips.

When I was working at Canal College, I also started attending group meetings for young people. So I ended up having two new things at the same time and I went from having nothing in my life to having no time to myself. That happened in the span of a couple of weeks. So it was a really big change and although it was really uncomfortable, I don't know, it's weird, I kind of got this pleasure out of it; like I don't really like it, but I'm doing it, if that makes sense? One thing I could never ever do was talk in front of people, and now I do it in college all the time, so that's something I never thought I'd be good at.

Before Canal College, I think I was getting to the point where I was going to give up, depression was getting hold of me and I just wasn't coping. I really do not ever want to relive those couple of years. Don't get me wrong, when I first started Canal College, I did have relapses of panic attacks, but I did eventually overcome them. I actually went on a skiing holiday with some of the people from my meeting group and I never would have done that before.

In three or four years I will be at university, I'm not sure which one yet. And probably at that time I'll be living in a flat with flatmates, probably have a good few pals and hopefully have a job at the same time.

My take on willpower is an image of someone about to bungee jump and you have to be the one to step off. Not so much ignoring the fear, but acknowledging it's there and accepting you've got to overcome it."

An insightful example of willpower from Abby, who has turned her life around using incredible self-control when she could have easily given up. There were many examples of willpower ingredients in her story. All of which we will explore further to help your own Willpower Challenges.

WILLPOWER INGREDIENTS IN ABBY'S STORY

- Abby's Challenge had huge *meaning* for her. It was a chance for a new start, a life.
- She said throughout, "I don't like it but I'm doing it!" With a Willpower Challenge you may have to accept that if you are entering an entirely new arena, you might be *uncomfortable* initially but that this will fade.
- She talked about her *goals* and they were very specific. Having clear goals is essential to willpower.
- She had a *clear vision* of how her future would look. Visualising success is a willpower skill.
- And she also provided a great example of *generalisation*: when she faced one hurdle she then felt she could take on others in the same way at the same time.
- She had a strong *belief* that all would work out.
- She provided a great example of the *three-week rule* to establish a new behaviour. After three weeks she was talking to others, not waiting for them to talk to her.

All these willpower ingredients will be at your disposal throughout the book.

Before we go any further, I would like you to assess your own willpower. I always like to begin an exploration of a topic with self-discovery. Let's not define willpower yet until you answer the questions and score the results; then we can build up a sense of what willpower entails.

DIRECTIONS FOR COMPLETING THE WILLPOWER SCALE

Table 1.1 lists a number of statements that may or may not apply to you. For the most accurate score, when responding, think of how you compare to most people – not just the people you know well, but most people in general. There are no right or wrong answers, so be brutally honest with yourself.

TABLE 1.1 The Willpower Scale

	Not like me at all	Not much like me	Somewhat like me	Mostly like me	Very much like me
1. I am good at resisting temptation					
2. I have a hard time breaking bad habits					
3. I have a tendency to be lazy					
4. I am flexible and open to change					
5. I tend to blurt things out					
6. I never overdo it when eating and drinking					
7. I do things that are bad for me if they are fun					
8. I wish I had more self-discipline					
9. I work really hard					
10. Sometimes I can't stop myself doing something even if I know it's wrong					

	Not like me at all	Not much like me	Somewhat like me	Mostly like me	Very much like me
11. I never act without thinking through alternatives					
12. I am able to work towards long-term goals					
13. Pleasure and fun sometimes get in the way of work being done					
14. People would say I have iron self-discipline					
15. I really learn from my mistakes					
16. I don't care if I'm different from other people					
17. I give up on things quickly					
18. I like things to remain the same					
19. I tend to fit in with the people around me					
20. I have a lot of willpower					

THE WILLPOWER SCALE

Scoring

To score the questionnaire, add up all the points that you have given to each of the questions. Write the totals in the boxes given here.

Results

1. For questions 1, 4, 6, 9, 11, 12, 14, 15, 16, 17 and 20 assign the following points:
   5 = Very much like me
   4 = Mostly like me
   3 = Somewhat like me
   2 = Not much like me
   1 = Not like me at all

	1	4	6	9	11	12	14	15	16	20
Total										

2. For questions 2, 3, 5, 7, 8, 10, 13, 17, 18 and 19 assign the following points:
   1 = Very much like me
   2 = Mostly like me
   3 = Somewhat like me
   4 = Not much like me
   5 = Not like me at all

	2	3	5	7	8	10	13	17	18	19
Total										

Add up all your points. The maximum score on this scale is 100 (high willpower), and the lowest scale on this scale is 20 (low willpower).

Willpower is About
- Resisting temptation in order to reach a desired goal.
- Establishing a useful habit or routine.
- Hard work to achieve good outcomes.
- A desire to change.
- Self-control over what you say and do.
- An ability to think through alternative ways of behaving.
- Not worrying what others think or do.

Results

If you achieved between *20* and *45* then this result constitutes a *low willpower score* and you will have considerable work to do on your willpower. You may consistently have trouble resisting temptation and will give in especially if those around you are doing so. You will tend to go for immediate rewards instead of delaying gratification to reach a goal.

A score of between *45* and *75* is a *medium willpower score* and you will have some successes but also some challenges. Review the scale and list all questions where you achieved a score of a 1, 2 or 3. These will be the areas which have undermined your willpower in the past and should be addressed for future success.

If you scored between *75* and *100* then this signifies a *high willpower score*. Well done. You tend to have good self-control, can generally resist temptation and have an ability to delay gratification. Unless you achieved a score of 100 then you may still have some work to do on certain aspects of willpower. Review the results and work out what aspects may require some improvement. You may also like to embrace a new Willpower Challenge in the future or help someone else with theirs, and this book provides the skills for both.

I'm not sure you would ever want to score 100, as self-control max may be an uncomfortable place to be!

Willpower covers a multitude of concepts and vocabulary and, as you will discover, it contains all of the ingredients you can see in Figure 1.1. We will explore them all throughout the book.

I have been a psychologist for more years than I care to mention and have spent my professional life helping clients develop successful strategies

FIGURE 1.1 The Ingredients of Willpower

and useful habits to achieve their goals, whatever they might be. Will-power is an intrinsic part of this change process and is a current focus of study, with much research surrounding the results of having it and the effects of not.

Let's take a look at some of this research before you embark on your own Willpower Challenge. You need to know what works and the research will guide you through the practicalities. It also helps you understand the importance of willpower when you want to change anything, a bad to a good habit, healthy eating, an exercise regime or indeed how you work.

WILLPOWER RESEARCH

"If only I had more willpower" is a cry heard often in the face of a diet jetti-soned, smoking restarted or any short-term pleasure pursued to the detri-ment of future gain. Is willpower an innate capability – something we just have or haven't – or is it something we can learn? I strongly believe the latter and yet those with great self-control often believe it is innate. They seem to feel as if they have always had it. Innate or learned, whichever you believe, willpower is certainly important.

The results of the American Psychological Association's annual *Stress in America* survey in 2011 revealed that 27% of participants cited a lack of willpower as the major reason they couldn't make healthy lifestyle changes.

In 2005, University of Pennsylvania psychologists Angela Duckworth and Martin Seligman explored self-control in school children over the course of a school year. The researchers first gauged the students' self-discipline (willpower) by having teachers, parents and the students themselves rate their behaviour.

They also gave students a task in which they had the option of receiving $1 immediately or waiting a week to receive $2. They found students who ranked high on self-discipline had better grades, better school attend-ance and were more likely to be admitted to a good high school. The clincher of the study was that willpower was more important than intel-ligence in predicting academic success. Wow.

Other studies have produced similar results. In 2004, June Tangney of George Mason University asked undergraduate students to complete self-control measures. They found that high self-control scores correlated with higher grade point averages, higher self-esteem, less binge-eating and alcohol abuse, and . . . would you believe it . . . better relationship skills. So a bit of self-control when providing feedback to your "other half" is fervently desired!

The benefits of willpower seem to extend well beyond school, college or university years. Terrie Moffitt of Duke University published results in 2011 about self-control in a group of 1000 individuals who were tracked from birth to 32 as part of a long-term health study in New Zealand. She and her colleagues found those with high self-control in childhood (as reported by teachers, parents and the children themselves) grew into adults with greater physical and mental health, fewer substance abuse problems and criminal convictions, better savings behaviour and greater financial security. Those patterns were nothing to do with family socio-economic status or, indeed, intelligence.

So willpower has huge general importance in nearly all areas of life.

> **Definition 1** Willpower is the ability to resist short-term temptations in order to meet long-term goals.

Before bringing things up to date, we first have to return to 1989 when Walter Mischel's research began. Mischel, a psychologist from Columbia University, explored self-control in children using the now famous "marshmallow test" and laid the groundwork for our understanding of self-control.

Young children were presented with a plate of marshmallows and invited to eat one. They were then told that the researcher would leave the room for a few minutes and if they waited until the researcher returned, they could eat two marshmallows. If the child couldn't wait for the returning researcher, they could ring a bell and the researcher would return but with no second marshmallow on offer.

The children with good self-control gave up the immediate pleasure of one in order to eat two at some later stage. Dieters resist chocolate cake so they can become more streamlined. Shoppers resist splurging at the mall so they can save for a comfortable retirement. All examples of resistance.

Actions for Willpower
· Remind yourself of the advantages of resistance. Write them down somewhere noticeable.
· Imagine the positive outcome. More money in the bank, a thinner you, two marshmallows not one.
· Distraction works. Look away from temptation. Do something else, anything else, just not what you want to avoid.

Mischel then proposed what he calls a "hot/cool" system to explain why willpower succeeds or fails. The cool system is cognitive and rational. It's a thinking system with knowledge about the impact of your choice with thoughts, feelings and actions all designed to remind you why you should leave the marshmallow where it belongs. While the cool system is relaxed, the hot system is impulsive and emotional. It is responsible for quick, knee-jerk responses to certain triggers, such as eating the marshmallow (and possibly the rest of the plate) immediately without thinking of the long-term implications.

When willpower fails, exposure to a "hot" stimulus essentially overrides the cool system, leading to impulsive actions. Some people, it seems, may be more or less susceptible to hot triggers. And that susceptibility to emotional responses may influence their behaviour throughout life, as Mischel discovered when he revisited his marshmallow-test subjects as adolescents. He found that teenagers who had waited longer for the marshmallows as young children were more likely to score higher on exams, and their parents were more likely to rate them as having a greater planning ability, handling stress well, showing self-control in frustrating situations and concentrating without becoming distracted.

As it turns out, the marshmallow study didn't end there. Bringing things up to date, B.J. Casey, of Weill Cornell Medical College, along with Mischel and Shoda of the University of Washington and other colleagues, tracked down 59 subjects, now in their 40s, who had participated in the marshmallow experiments as children. The researchers tested the subjects' willpower strength again with different measures (not marshmallows!).

Amazingly, the subjects' willpower differences had mostly been maintained over four decades. In general, children who were less successful at resisting the marshmallow all those years ago did less well on the self-control task as adults. An individual's sensitivity to so-called "hot stimuli", it seems, may continue throughout their life.

Additionally, Casey and her colleagues examined brain activity in some subjects using functional magnetic resonance imaging. When presented with tempting stimuli, individuals with low self-control showed brain patterns that differed from those with high self-control. The researchers found that the prefrontal cortex (a region in the brain that controls functions, such as making decisions) was more active in subjects with higher self-control. And the ventral striatum (a region thought to be involved in desires and rewards) showed boosted activity in those with lower self-control.

So what is happening in our brains when faced with willpower? And can "hot" choice people "un-happen" this response and become "cool"? I started to pursue these thoughts by looking at the brain, as it seems to me that this is the nub of our understanding about willpower.

Definition 2 Willpower is cool and rational.

WILLPOWER IS A GAME OF TWO BRAINS

Contrary to the thoughts of Plato and Freud, plus other advocates of the rationality of man, it was discovered that if we didn't have emotion, reason would go out the window. This resulted from assessment of patients with frontal lobe brain damage. The outcome was that despite retaining all intellectual faculties these patients couldn't make a decision. They had become unemotional and were simply overwhelmed with detail as all options in their lives had the same weight. We make choices with feelings. So contrary to Plato, who thought that pure reason was devoid of emotion, in fact nothing could be further from the truth . . . and this was in the frontal cortex, traditionally thought to be the home of higher-order rational thought.

It was once thought that the complexity of function rose as you went up the levels. Figure 1.2 categorises these functions from animalistic brainstem to the abstract thinking of the frontal cortex. The reality is even more complex, with many links from the lower three levels to the frontal cortex.

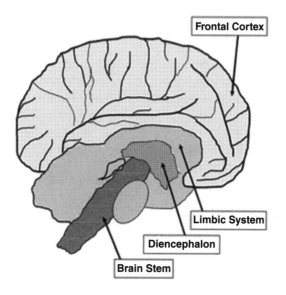

Frontal Cortex

Limbic System

Diencephalon

Brain Stem

FIGURE 1.2 The Four Levels in the Brain

There are four levels in the brain starting with the *brain stem,* which regu-
lates our bodily functions of temperature, breathing and heart-beat, then
the *diencephalon* which is involved in hunger and sleep. The *limbic system*
is the third level and the centre for emotions of violence, lust and impulsive, animalistic behaviour. And then the fourth upper level of the brain
the *frontal cortex,* traditionally viewed as the source of intelligence and
rationality (see Figure 1.2).

It was believed that as the functions rose from brainstem to frontal cortex –
like an elevator in a store passing through a variety of departments – they
became increasingly higher order: from the sub-basement of animalistic
instinct to the top floor of conceptual thought (Figure 1.3).

Simply put, the idea was that the top floor development of the frontal
cortex placed us humans above any other animal as it emphasised our
rationality and was our differentiator, our evolutionary USP. This was
wrong!

The frontal cortex **is** involved with emotion, connecting the lower three
levels with the upper-level thought processes. In particular it is the orbito-
frontal cortex which integrates emotion into our decision-making process. And it is this link to our lower, older animal brain which allows us
to make speedy decisions based on previous encounters and learning.

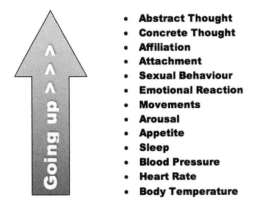

- **Abstract Thought**
- **Concrete Thought**
- **Affiliation**
- **Attachment**
- **Sexual Behaviour**
- **Emotional Reaction**
- **Movements**
- **Arousal**
- **Appetite**
- **Sleep**
- **Blood Pressure**
- **Heart Rate**
- **Body Temperature**

FIGURE 1.3 Elevator Brain

In fact, we need both the upper and lower brains to make decisions. So the sub-basement has all sorts of back stairs to the top floors of our brains!

This system worked particularly well when we were emerging from the jungle, walking erect and on the lookout for predators. The advantage of our evolutionary brains was that we kept the animal brain as well as our higher-order brain and, when threatened by something hairier and larger than we were, this lower brain kicked in – overriding the higher-order thinking brain. Dopamine, the "surprise" neurotransmitter, is launched from our mid brains putting us on high alert.

This fight or flight stress response – with beating heart, rapid breathing and all senses alert – ensures that we mobilise quickly. Stress hormones are released from the adrenal glands along with fats and sugar from our liver, lungs pump to fuel the body with extra oxygen and our cardiovascular system is in high gear to provide energy to fight this thing or run as fast as we can. And all of this happens quicker than a click of the fingers. Left up to the frontal lobes of the upper brain we would still be contemplating what to do and become a beast's lunch. End of species!

For our purposes here, willpower is often a struggle, sometimes daily, between our higher-order first-level brain – the prefrontal cortex – and the impulsivity of our second-level brain which houses the limbic system with links to the ventral striatum, as mentioned by Casey and others in their post-marshmallow research. Let me give another example.

We have now eschewed the jungle for a more modern lifestyle and we socialise after work. We have a goal to drink less alcohol as our weekly intake has been going over healthy limits. We are in a bar after work with our friends who have ordered a bottle of wine and poured a glass for us. We reach out a hand to pick up the glass as if powered by an alien source. "But wait a minute, I am not drinking alcohol, I've made that promise to myself and my liver." What is going on the brain in anticipation of that first sip? Well that neurotransmitter dopamine pings again with surprise but this time also with the promise of reward. Heart rate increases, blood pressure goes up. You want that drink and the others are having a great time and you don't want to be the odd one out drinking water! But at the same time you also know that you had a goal to drink less. You are under threat – not from a large hairy beast but from the internal conflict you are experiencing. The game of two brains for a modern threat! Fight or flight is not appropriate here: who do you fight, except yourself, and where do you run to?

Psychologist Suzanne Segerstrom from the University of Kentucky has studied the effects of self-control on mind and body and how we can learn to resist temptation. She calls this *pause and plan*, the absolute reverse of fight or flight.

Pause and plan starts with the realisation that you have a two-brain conflict. You know you shouldn't have that glass of wine as you promised yourself, but you really, really want it. You need help at this point to ward off a potentially bad decision.

Enter willpower. The prefrontal cortex jumps in wearing a Superman outfit and helps you to make the good, beneficial choice. Pause then plan. Relax, take a deep breath, perhaps move away and think what to do. Slow things down. Order an alcohol free beer and offer your glass of wine to a friend. Pause and plan offers freedom from the terrorism of your lower brain.

Just to reiterate, the *prefrontal cortex* is the cerebral cortex which covers the front part of the frontal lobe. There is an integral link between a person's personality and the functions of the prefrontal cortex. This brain region has been implicated in planning complex cognitive behaviour, personality expressiveness, decision making and moderating social behaviour. This relates to our ability to differentiate conflicting thoughts, future consequences of our behaviour, working towards a defined goal, prediction of outcomes, expectation based on actions and social control (the ability to suppress urges that might be embarrassing). This is sounding like the home of willpower.

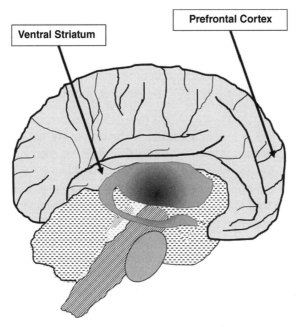

FIGURE 1.4 Upper and Lower Brain

But then we have the *ventral striatum* which is interconnected with the limbic system lower brain (see Figure 1.4). It's believed to have involvement in motor movement as well as emotional responses, particularly those related to pleasure and behavioural motivation.

So this is why the marshmallow leavers had activity in the prefrontal cortex and the marshmallow eaters had activity in the ventral striatum. The former – designated the "cool" people – paused and decided; whereas the latter – "hot" responders – impulsively ate. A long explanation to come to this understanding; however, it has huge significance for willpower. Can this response be undone? Absolutely.

Actions for Willpower
When confronted by temptation:

- Be cool.
- Pause and take a deep breath.
- Put some distance between you and the desired "thing".
- Plan an alternative strategy.
- Remember why you want to resist temptation.

Let's hear from a willpower star describing his view of this upper and lower brain conflict.

Todd Whiteford was diagnosed with testicular cancer. Between surgery and chemotherapy, he decided to run the Marathon des Sables, the most difficult land race in the world. Here he describes the meaning of willpower for him.

> *"My example of lack of willpower is knowing you're not meant to eat bad stuff because you're training for a race and then just eating bad stuff anyway. Always a challenge. I think it is a lot to do with determination and harnessing your brain's capability to make your physical body just do what you want. And I think if you look at the endurance types in sport, it's about the power of the mind over what you perceive your muscles can do. So in the Tour De France, for example, these guys are in pain, but they know that they can tell themselves that the pain is only temporary and they need to endure it to get to where they want to be. And I think that's willpower. It's the ability to override what your physical body is telling you, that you're in pain or you should stop or you're tired. Willpower is the mind's ability to override those feelings for something bigger or better.*

Definition 3 Willpower is the override switch of the upper brain over the lower.

The glorious outcome recent research has provided is that the brain is not fixed but learns from experience and practice. London taxi drivers, for instance, develop density of grey matter in the spatial awareness part of the brain as they take their "knowledge" exams. Do something every day and your brain is enhanced. I remember playing table tennis every day in my sixth year at school and my reaction times in general speeded up exponentially. There were probably other, better things I could have practised, but hey ho. So we can also train ourselves for higher self-control.

The best way to do this is by learning to meditate, as pause and plan works so much better when we are calm. With even short spells of meditation there is increased blood flow to the prefrontal cortex – the home of decision making. Eight to twelve hours of meditation increases neural connections, which help us stay focused on controlling impulses and increasing concentration. Grey matter actually increases in the prefrontal cortex.

We will explore the skills of meditation and relaxation later in the book.

Can we overdo willpower and exhaust ourselves? Let's take a look at some of the research that has been the foundation of previous thinking about willpower.

WILLPOWER IS A LIMITED RESOURCE . . . OR IS IT?

Although Mischel's hot–cool concept may explain our ability to delay our marshmallow eating, another theory known as willpower depletion emerged to explain what happens after we've resisted multiple temptations.

Every day we make decisions and exert willpower. We resist the urge to search the internet for the best holiday deals instead of finishing a work report. We reach for a salad when we're craving a fish supper, shut up when we'd like to make a snide remark. Yet some research shows that resisting repeated temptations takes a mental toll. Some experts liken willpower to a muscle that can get fatigued from overuse.

Some of the earliest evidence of this effect came from the lab of Roy Baumeister in 1998. He brought subjects into a room filled with the aroma of freshly baked cookies. The table before them held a plate of the cookies and a bowl of radishes. Some subjects were asked to sample the cookies, while others were asked to eat the radishes. Afterwards, they were given 30 minutes to complete a difficult geometric puzzle.

Baumeister and his colleagues found that people who ate radishes as asked and resisted the cookies gave up on the puzzle after about 8 minutes, while the cookie-eaters persevered for nearly 19 minutes on average. Drawing on willpower to resist the cookies, it seemed, drained the subjects' self-control for subsequent situations.

I have to say I was always a bit suspicious of these results. If I were in the radish group, I would have been profoundly annoyed and irritated with the subsequent task!

Since that work was published in 1998, numerous studies have built a case for willpower depletion, or "ego" depletion as some experts call it. In one example, volunteers who were asked to suppress their feelings as they viewed an emotional movie gave up sooner on a test of physical stamina than did volunteers who watched the film reacting normally. In another, people who actively suppressed certain thoughts were less able to stifle their laughter in a follow-up test designed to make them giggle.

Dealing with a hostile audience (or your in-laws) may feel exhausting, but depletion is not simply a matter of being tired, as Vohs demonstrated. She subjected half of her study subjects to 24 hours of sleep deprivation before asking them to suppress their emotional reactions to a film clip. Then she tested the subjects' self-control strength. To her surprise, she found that the subjects who'd been up all night were no more likely to become willpower-depleted than those who'd spent the night snug in their beds.

So if depletion isn't physical fatigue, what is it? Recent investigations have found a number of possible mechanisms for willpower depletion, including some at a biological level. Scientists at the University of Toronto found that people whose willpower was depleted by self-control tasks showed decreased activity in the anterior cingulate cortex, a brain region involved with cognition. When your willpower has been tested, your brain may actually function differently.

Other evidence suggests that willpower-depleted individuals might be low on fuel. The brain is a high-energy organ, powered by a steady supply of glucose (blood sugar). Some researchers have proposed that brain cells working hard to maintain self-control consume glucose faster than it can be replenished. In a study lending support to this idea, obedient dogs made to resist temptation had lower blood-glucose levels than dogs that did not exert self-control.

Studies in humans have found similar patterns. Human subjects who exerted willpower in lab tasks had lower glucose levels than control subjects who weren't asked to draw on their self-control. Furthermore, restoring glucose appears to help reboot run-down willpower. One study, for example, found that drinking sugar-sweetened lemonade restored willpower strength in depleted individuals, while drinking sugar-free lemonade did not.

NEW RESEARCH TO CHALLENGE WILLPOWER AS A LIMITED RESOURCE

Now, a team led by Evan Carter at the University of Miami has argued that these studies were seriously flawed and has published their own series of meta-analyses, the findings of which undermine the limited resource theory.

The new meta-analysis considers the combined results from many studies following this format, but the new analyses are far stricter in that they only consider studies that used tasks well-established in the literature as ways to challenge willpower, including suppressing emotional reactions to videos and resisting tempting food, and that also used established tasks as outcome measures, including persistence on impossible anagrams, food consumption and standardised academic tests.

Carter and his team trawled conference reports to find unpublished studies on willpower. This is important because in this scientific field, as in most others, it's likely that there has been a bias in the literature towards publishing positive results (in this case, those consistent with the popular idea that willpower becomes depleted with repeated use).

When Carter's team analysed the evidence from the 68 relevant published and 48 relevant unpublished studies that they identified, they found very little overall support for the idea that willpower is a limited resource. It's worth noting too that there are recent doubts raised about a related idea in willpower research – the notion that depleted self-control is caused by a lack of sugar in the body. So no excuse for those sweets on your desk while you are completing that deadline report.

The new analyses even found some support for the idea that self-control improves through successive challenges, a result that's consistent with the concept of generalisation that Abby – our Canal volunteer – evidenced when she threw herself into a number of new areas requiring willpower at the same time and was hugely successful.

Finally, I discovered an article by Melissa Dahl in March 2016 which declared that if you believe that your willpower is limitless, then it is. I investigated further. What if you happened to be someone who believed that engaging in difficult tasks was *energising*, like Abby at Canal College, rather than depleting? What if you held a belief that using your willpower activates your reserves, like Todd, rather than drains them? What would happen?

A new set of studies by Veronika Job, Carol Dweck and Gregory Walton – entitled "Ego Depletion – Is It All in Your Head?" in the *Journal for the Association of Psychological Science*, in 2010 – revealed that people's beliefs about the nature of self-control determine whether or not willpower is depleted by use.

The researchers distinguished between people who believed willpower is a limited resource or an unlimited resource, and found that only those who believed in the limited-resource theory had less self-control and made mistakes after working on something very difficult.

How can this be? Both groups were equally exhausted by the difficult task, so you might think they would be equally mistake-prone. But it turns out that our personal theories about self-control determine how exhaustion affects us.

When people who hold the limited-resource view experience something as exhausting, they have less self-control and are more prone to errors because they see exhaustion as a sign to reduce effort, so they can rest and eventually replenish their self-control reserves. In contrast, folk with the unlimited-resource view keep going despite their exhaustion, and make fewer errors because of it.

These beliefs, not surprisingly, predict how people handle the more stressful and demanding periods in their lives. For instance, the researchers found that during the more stressful, exam-filled weeks in the academic semester, belief in the limited-resource theory of self-control predicted greater consumption of unhealthy junk foods, procrastination and less-effective study habits among college students. Those who believed in limitless willpower, on the other hand, held up under stress just fine.

So, is self-control limited or isn't it? The answer has become a lot less clear and, frankly, I'm no longer sure it matters. What **does** matter is whether or not you believe that it's limited. And since you have some choice when it comes to your beliefs, I recommend going with the limitless willpower view. Maybe, in the end, all it takes to put down that packet of biscuits is believing that you actually can. And if you know you can with the biscuits, then what else could you do? You are then on a willpower trajectory.

So the concept of willpower being like a muscle with all the limitations of a muscle – like overuse or depletion – is questionable. A much better working concept is that willpower is a *mindset* and limitless.

> **Definition 4** Willpower is a mindset and therefore limitless!

To finish this first part of *Willpower*, let me introduce *Mark Masson*. He discusses his fight with cancer, what his mindset was like during this time and what he felt helped him.

MARK MASSON ON WILLPOWER AND HEALTH

"I was diagnosed with advanced Hodgkin's lymphoma and had countless cocktails of therapies, medications, radiotherapy sessions, and they weren't really working, I had relapses and a bone marrow transplant and more relapses and then I was told nothing more could be done and I was given an estimated survival time of a year.

I then looked around worldwide for other treatments and ended up with what at the time was a pretty experimental donor bone marrow transplant. And, well, since I'm alive and speaking to you, it worked. So after that kind of transplant, it's a long recovery time. Your whole body has to regain strength, so for between eight to ten years I was just out of the world.

In terms of willpower – I think I definitely have it because I know the steps I took every day, the small goals I set mentally to force myself to be able to say if I don't make it, I've done my best. The last thing I ever want to do is preach, because if the medicine hadn't worked, regardless of how hard I'd tried with willpower, without the medicine I wouldn't have survived. After recovering I moved back to London with my family, I set up a business and I've now got my life back.

I can't overestimate the amount of mental force that you actually need to fight and recover. There's a very interesting equation that I learned empirically: you need an absolute desire and drive to come through it with utter focus, while at the same time finding a way to be at peace. When you're told you're not going to live, you need to get to an area of peace or else you just torture your mind while it's also hell on earth physically. I just hate failing; that is a driver for me. I like the feeling of success so for me willpower is just a very basic, man-with-a-spear kind of a driver."

REMINDERS

- To exercise willpower, you require a meaningful goal, one that is meaningful to you; for example, going to university, a physically or mentally stretching challenge, staying alive.
- Self-control is the upper "cool" rational brain fighting the pleasure-principled, instant gratification "hot" lower brain and winning.
- Use pause and plan at every opportunity. Distract yourself and give yourself time to think of alternative strategies.
- Be prepared to put up with a lack of comfort in new or unusual circumstances, knowing that this will pass.
- Learn to relax as relaxation improves everything . . . well almost everything. Be at peace. Instructions to follow in Part Four.
- Start to believe that willpower works. Start to believe that your willpower works.
- Begin to feel a drive for success.

PART TWO

Goals and Vision

Part One provided understanding about the science of willpower and the personal impact of willpower on lives. Part Two gets active and is all about goal planning and visualising success for your own Willpower Challenge.

Without goals you are unfocused and the chance of being successful is severely reduced. So, before embarking on your Willpower Challenge, let's look at the purpose of goals and then assess your goal planning skills.

WHY GOALS?

You can have all the potential in the world but without focus your abilities and talent are useless. In the way that sunlight can't burn through anything without a magnifying glass, you can't achieve anything unless a goal is focusing your effort. Goals are what give you direction in life, and by setting goals you provide a target. This sense of direction is what allows your mind to focus and, rather than waste energy shooting aimlessly, allows you to hit your target and reach your goal.

By setting goals you are also able to measure your progress because you have a fixed endpoint. My Willpower Challenge was to complete the book *Willpower* in six months. Starting in January, I had to plan my reading, interviewing and data collation well before I put pen to paper, finger to computer. Having this project mapped out over a finite time period has been hugely motivational.

Goals also provide mental boundaries. When you have an end point in mind you stay away from distractions and remain focused on the goal. Some preparation, like telling friends and family what you are trying to achieve, is very useful so that you can avoid tempting offers of drinks, suppers or other entertainments.

When you set a goal you make yourself accountable to finishing the task. This is in contrast with when you do things spontaneously and it doesn't really matter whether you complete the task or not. Goals tend to stick in your mind, especially if they are written down or reminders are set in your diary, and if not completed they give you a jolt. All this helps to overcome procrastination and laziness.

If a deadline is three months away, divide it into several short-term goals so you can complete a piece of the larger long-term goal every week or even every day. Diary it in, lest you forget.

The underpinning of getting anything done is based on goals. Goal setting provides the foundation for drive and with a goal in mind you can visualise success and imagine how that might feel. Goals propel you forward, providing a sense of speed and direction.

Remember: there will always be conflicting goals. If you have the goal of getting fit and have committed to run every day, another goal will vie with the first. It's the sit-on-the-couch-and-watch-television goal. If you want to lose weight by eating a healthy diet, there will be the accompanying goal of wanting to eat a plate of chips which you love.

Willpower is choosing the long-term "good for you" goal over short-term temptation of "the bad for you" goal.

But how successful are you in all aspects of goal setting, planning and implementation? I have simplified the established SRQ – Self Regulation Questionnaire – developed by Brown, Miller and Lawendowski in 1999. The two underlying factors tested here are *goal setting* and *implementation*.

So, complete *The Goals Questionnaire*, and after scoring you will discover the areas which you need to improve to reach your goals.

Goals Questionnaire

Please answer the following questions by circling the response that best describes how you are. If you STRONGLY DISAGREE with a statement, circle 1. If you DISAGREE circle 2. If you are UNCERTAIN or UNSURE circle 3. If you AGREE circle 4 and if you STRONGLY AGREE circle 5. There are no right or wrong answers. Work quickly and don't think too long about your answers.

1. I usually keep track of my progress toward my goals	1 2 3 4 5
2. I give up on my goals too easily	1 2 3 4 5 R
3. I doubt I could change even if I wanted to	1 2 3 4 5 R
4. I get easily distracted from my plans	1 2 3 4 5 R
5. I reward myself for progress toward my goals	1 2 3 4 5
6. I don't notice the effects of my actions until it's too late	1 2 3 4 5 R
7. It's hard for me to see anything helpful about changing my ways	1 2 3 4 5 R
8. I am able to accomplish goals I set for myself	1 2 3 4 5
9. I put off making decisions	1 2 3 4 5 R
10. I have so many plans that it's hard for me to focus on any one of them	1 2 3 4 5 R
11. I change the way I do things when I see a problem with how things are going	1 2 3 4 5
12. It's hard for me to notice when I've had enough alcohol, food or sweets	1 2 3 4 5 R
13. I am willing to consider other ways of doing things	1 2 3 4 5
14. If I want to change, I am confident I could do it	1 2 3 4 5
15. When it comes to deciding about a change, I feel overwhelmed by the choices	1 2 3 4 5 R
16. I have trouble following through with things once I've made up my mind to do something	1 2 3 4 5 R
17. I can stick to a plan that's working well	1 2 3 4 5
18. I usually only have to make a mistake in order to learn from it	1 2 3 4 5
19. I am set in my ways	1 2 3 4 5 R
20. As soon as I see a problem, I start looking for possible solutions	1 2 3 4 5
21. I have a hard time setting goals for myself	1 2 3 4 5 R

(Continued)

22. When I'm trying to change something, I pay a lot of attention to how I'm doing	1 2 3 4 5
23. I usually judge how I'm doing by the consequences of my actions	1 2 3 4 5
24. As soon as I see things aren't going well, I want to do something about it	1 2 3 4 5
25. There is usually more than one way to accomplish something	1 2 3 4 5
26. I have trouble making plans to help me reach my goals	1 2 3 4 5 R
27. I set goals for myself and keep track of my progress	1 2 3 4 5
28. Most of the time I don't pay attention to what I'm doing	1 2 3 4 5 R
29. I tend to keep doing the same thing, even when it doesn't work	1 2 3 4 5 R
30. Once I have a goal, I can usually plan how to reach it	1 2 3 4 5
31. I have rules that I stick to no matter what	1 2 3 4 5 R
32. If I make a resolution to change something, I pay a lot of attention to how I'm doing	1 2 3 4 5
33. Often I don't notice what I'm doing until someone calls it to my attention	1 2 3 4 5 R
34. I am very spontaneous about my goals	1 2 3 4 5 R
35. Usually I see the need to change before others do	1 2 3 4 5
36. I'm good at finding different ways to get what I want	1 2 3 4 5
37. I usually think before I act	1 2 3 4 5
38. Little problems or distractions throw me off course	1 2 3 4 5 R
39. I learn from my mistakes when I am pursuing my goals	1 2 3 4 5
40. I know how I want to be	1 2 3 4 5
41. It bothers me when things aren't the way I want them	1 2 3 4 5
42. I call on others for help when I need it	1 2 3 4 5
43. Before making a decision, I consider what is likely to happen	1 2 3 4 5
44. I tend to give up on my goals quickly	1 2 3 4 5 R
45. I usually decide to change and hope for the best	1 2 3 4 5 R
46. I write down my goals	1 2 3 4 5
47. I'm very motivated to achieve my goals	1 2 3 4 5
48. I see things through to the end	1 2 3 4 5

Calculating Your Results

1. With questions that are marked with an R, reverse the scale to score your points – see below:
   1 = strongly agree
   2 = agree
   3 = uncertain
   4 = disagree
   5 = strongly disagree

2. Now add all your points for all questions on Figure 2.1, and total each of the six sections and then add together to get a total for goal planning and implementation. Finally add both together to get an overall score.

	Goal Planning									
1	Planning	9	15	21	26	30	37	43	46	Total
2	Personal Change	2	7	13	19	24	35	40	41	Total
3	Motivation	3	8	14	20	25	36	42	47	Total
				Total for Goal Planning						
	Implementation									
4	Feedback	1	6	12	23	28	33	34	39	Total
5	Action	4	10	16	17	31	38	44	48	Total
6	Assessing	5	11	18	22	27	29	32	45	Total
				Total for Implementation						
				Overall Total						

FIGURE 2.1 Goal Planning

Total Score:

between *161* and *240* denotes *high* planning and implementation capacity and a good ability to reach goals

between *113* and *160* means that you have an *intermediate* (moderate) planning and implementation capacity and may not reach all of your goals

between *48* and *112* is a score at the *bottom end*, revealing a low (impaired) planning and implementation capacity and a severely diminished chance of reaching your goals.

Now review the scores for each of the six sections and discover where your strengths lie and where you might require support or back up.

Many people who are good at *goal planning,* who enjoy the notion of personal change and are really motivated, can be poor at the follow through of self-regulation: implementation, feedback and assessment of progress.

For those of you who are magnificent at *implementation* and have a spreadsheet at the ready to chart their progress at every turn, you may require motivation to get started. You often wait for the perfect moment which may never arrive!

The key take away from this questionnaire is that you need goal planning *and* implementation to succeed.

If you are tackling your Willpower Challenge alone, I would suggest asking for support – especially with the parts of goal planning or implementation that you might find tedious but could be exciting for others to help you.

GOAL PLANNING

To inspire you with the success of goals, let me introduce you to *Jamie Andrew*'s extraordinary story and his Willpower Challenges. He became a quadruple amputee after being stuck in a storm while mountaineering in the Alps and has achieved wonderful things despite, or indeed because of, his special circumstances.

> *"It was in 1999 that my climbing partner and I went to climb Les Droits by its famous north face, and we were both very experienced mountaineers. We went to tackle the climb as a winter ascent which is the most serious time of the year to climb in the Alps, but we were*

well prepared for that kind of thing. So we did the climb in great conditions, but as we were approaching the summit on the second day that we were caught out by an unexpected and vicious storm which hadn't been forecast when we set out. So we did the sensible thing, we dug ourselves in, actually right on the summit of the mountain. We chiselled a ledge out of the mountain and settled down to sit it out, but unfortunately the storm lasted a great deal longer than we'd anticipated and we ended up being trapped on the summit of the mountain for a total of five days and five nights. And as those days progressed, it became more and more evident that we weren't going to get out of there alive ourselves and that a rescue became our best hope. But the conditions for the emergency services were just as challenging as they were for us. Sadly, by the time they did manage to affect a rescue on the morning of the fifth day, it was too late for my friend, who had died of hypothermia on the final night, and very nearly too late for me too. I was rescued, but I had to pay a very high price. My hands and feet were literally frozen solid by that stage and about a week later in hospital they had to be amputated.

I really learned about willpower when I was in hospital, unable to do anything for myself, and just having to take things one step at a time. Each morning I would just do something new; I would practise picking up a spoon or putting on a t shirt or learning to wash myself with a flannel or learning to walk on prosthetic legs.

And I realised the strength of that step-by-step process and also of relying on the support of everybody who wanted to help, and not going to my default position from before which was to be quite self-sufficient, proud and insular. In order to be self-sufficient, I had to rely on the support of other people. And that actually opened things up a lot too. So those two things really helped me put in mind a kind of method of taking on a challenge, whatever that challenge might be, and so when it came to going back to run a marathon or rock climbing or learning to ski again, I would just bear that in mind. I would say to myself, I'm just going to take this one step at a time. And, moreover, I'm not going to be put off or daunted by the enormity of a challenge, I'm just going to give it a go and find out what happens. So with the likes of skiing, I would just say, well I'm not quite sure how this is going to work, but I'm just going to put on a pair of ski boots and clip on a pair of skis and go skiing and see what happens, and in actual fact more often than not it would work.

So the dream goal is the aim, but before that there are many mid-term goals, which are big achievements but ones I might be able to reach monthly or yearly. But then equally important are those day-to-day goals. It really does help to write those goals down to be able to make sense of them in your head. And I think it's an approach that's tried and tested and really does work.

Failures turn out to be part of the learning experience; they're not failures so much as negative learning results and you move forward and try something different. Sometimes it can be hard having setbacks, but that's what life's all about."

Let's hear from *Todd Whiteford* again about goals. You met him in Part One, and if you remember he ran the Marathon de Sables after surgery for testicular cancer.

"Willpower for me comes from doing things in stages. So if we take the example of swimming, you set yourself a target and say, eventually I would like to be able to swim 100 lengths, then all you need to do is start and try one length, and the next day two. At first, it would feel like ten lengths would be a really difficult thing to do, but by then succeeding and then surpassing that, you're teaching your brain and your body that your mind is in control, because your mind is telling you to just keep going, and although you're in pain and think you should stop, you learn. You're teaching your body that things can be achieved. I used to think that doing five lengths was the most difficult thing ever, and now I'm up to seventy and five is nothing. You're changing and developing your goals as you go along. Setting incrementally more difficult goals as you achieve them. That's willpower."

Your own Willpower Challenges may be adventuring, like the heroes who have told us their stories, or might be giving up an unhealthy habit of smoking or eating the wrong diet. It could be deciding to go for promotion or becoming more relaxed, or like me writing *Willpower* in six months.

YOUR WILLPOWER GOALS

Write down the goals you would like to achieve for your Willpower Challenge. They may be part of the whole Challenge or separate Challenges. I don't think you will want to list more than three as you will need to focus your willpower. There may be one goal that stands out from the rest as being the most important, the one that might realise the largest difference or potential in your life.

Goal 1 _____

Goal 2 _____

Goal 3 _____

Looking at the list of goals, do any strike you as a priority or a key goal that if reached would secure the success of others? Rank your goals from one to three on their importance and plan to start on number one.

Now, with your goal at the top, add in the mini goals required to achieve it.

The goal can be your ultimate dream and the mini goals the daily or monthly tasks of how you get there. Think of Todd swimming one length or Jamie picking up a spoon; small steps towards getting to a much larger achievement. I have allowed three goals and three mini goals for each. You may have considerably more, but writing them down is the important part as it aids memory and increases commitment.

Goals and Mini Goals for Your Willpower Challenge

Goal 1 _____

_____

_____

Mini Goals _____

_____

_____

Goal 2 _____

_____

_____

Mini Goals _____

_____

_____

Goal 3 _____

_____

_____

Mini Goals _____

_____

_____

It is worth checking again at this stage that the goals you have set are things you really want to achieve, are meaningful to you and not ones at someone else's behest. It might be a dream goal of world peace – but what part of that is under your control to change? Many mini goals would be necessary for that one!

Goals and Mini Goals for My Willpower Challenge

Goal 1 _Willpower_ book written and delivered by 31 July: Mini goals

- Literature search – books and articles to be read between February and March
  - Two books and four journal articles per week
- Interviews carried out between March and May
  - Three interviews per week, transcribed and edited
- Five parts of the book written by mid-July
  - Parts One and Two by end of May
  - Parts Three and Four by end of June
  - Part Five by mid-July
- Editing last week of July

Goal 2 Swimming every day while finalising _Willpower_ in Lanzarote

Mini goals
- Week 1: 10 lengths of the pool
- Week 2: 20 lengths of the pool
- Week 3: 30 lengths of the pool

As you have seen in the _Goals Questionnaire_, you can be great at setting goals but not at following them through with self-regulation. So here is a _Goals Checklist_ as a daily reminder. This checklist covers feedback and assessment, so if that is a known weakness, place it in a prominent spot to be reviewed every day.

Goals Checklist

1. What did you do today to reach your goal?

_____

2. What got in the way?

_____

3. How did you deal with that? If positive, what did you do? If negative, what did you do?

_____

4. If you messed up or missed a deadline, what were your thoughts, feelings and actions?

_____

5. What is your learning from this?

_____

6. What might help tomorrow?

_____

7. What might you say to yourself that might help you resist temptation or stop an impulse to sabotage your goal?

_____

8. When in the day do you tend to give in? How could you avoid that?

_____

9. How much progress have you made so far on your goal? Circle the appropriate number, where 1 = "not much" and 10 = "a lot".

1	2	3	4	5	6	7	8	9	10

10. How committed are you now to your Willpower Challenge? Circle the appropriate number, where 1 = "not very" and 10 = "very much".

1	2	3	4	5	6	7	8	9	10

> If not committed, change your challenge.

The *Goals Checklist* is about planning for failure and about learning from inevitable glitches. This is so that you don't throw in the towel at the first hurdle but view any backsliding as part of the plan and get back with the programme.

It also acts as a reminder, as one of the major reasons you don't reach your goals is that you forget about them. Life takes over and goals are forgotten. Daily reminders of what you have achieved keep you on track.

Devise a short mantra to keep you on track. My mantra is "FOCUS FOCUS" as there are so many distractions in my life that I need constant reminders to stay on plan.

Finally, the self-awareness of knowing when you are vulnerable to backsliding or giving in to temptation means that you can plan distractions, replacement strategies or support from friends and family at those times.

Actions for Willpower
- Establish goals for your Willpower Challenge.
- Add mini goals, as outlining the steps to a goal increases success.
- Plan to fail so you have a back-up strategy should glitches occur in your plan.
- Keep daily reminders of your goals and mini goals in a prominent place.
- Create a mantra to keep you on track.

HOW YOU LEARN

When considering your Willpower Challenge, or indeed Challenges, you need to think about how you want to proceed. Is this a lone enterprise or one supported by or carried out with others? Is it something you need to research, or a very practical endeavour which just needs to be started?

When you are embarking on a difficult challenge it is worth knowing how best you learn to make life that bit easier. Any Willpower Challenge will involve learning. There are four learning styles, so to discover your style complete the Learning for Willpower Questionnaire here. Rate each question on a scale of 1 to 4 where 1 is least like you and 4 is most like you.

Learning for Willpower Questionnaire

	Rate each statement from 1 to 4 – 4 being most like you, 1 least like you – and place that number in the box.	
1	I see learning and knowledge as growth in personal insight	
2	I try to be as accurate as possible	
3	I thrive on plans and timelines	
4	I am interested in self-discovery	
5	I believe that information should be presented systematically	
6	I enjoy experiential learning	
7	I like to learn by example	
8	I learn by discussing ideas and facts with others	
9	I enjoy working in groups	
10	I like to be provided with skills to tackle problems	
11	When I learn I want variety in teaching and presentation methods	
12	I enjoy learning about facts and details	
13	Technical things and hands-on activities help me to learn	
14	I tackle problems by looking for patterns and possibilities	
15	Learning for me is about realistic feedback	
16	I tackle problems with rationality and logic	
17	I like to integrate knowledge into something new and boundary breaking	
18	Principles and procedures are important when in a learning situation	
19	I enjoy being supportive of others while they are learning	
20	When I am in a learning situation I want to see practical applications	
21	I thrive on developing good ideas	
22	I like to read about things in more depth	
23	I really seek quality, productivity and speed	
24	I seek to energise and be energised	

Rating Scale

Transfer your scores from the 24 questions in the Learning for Willpower Questionnaire to the table given here. The highest score for any question is 4 and the lowest 1. Now total your scores for each style.

Style 1		Style 2		Style 3		Style 4	
Question	Score	Question	Score	Question	Score	Question	Score
1		2		3		4	
8		5		7		6	
9		12		10		11	
15		16		13		14	
19		18		20		17	
21		22		23		24	
Total		Total		Total		Total	

To obtain a visual depiction of all four of your learning style scores, chart your scores on Your Learning Style Profile and join each score together. A sample profile is shown first to help.

Figure 2.2 shows a sample of a high Style 3 learner. Now chart your scores in Figure 2.3 to achieve your profile.

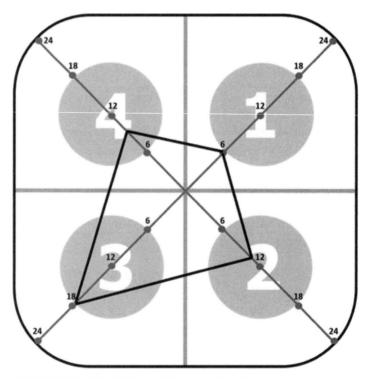

FIGURE 2.2 High Style 3 Learner Profile

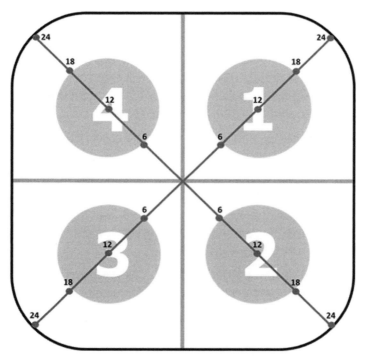

FIGURE 2.3 Your Willpower Learner Profile

Interpretation of Results

Style 1 learners have a strong preference for listening and discussing ideas. You learn best by relating new ideas to prior knowledge and personal experience. You thrive where there is respect for everyone's ideas and where people work together towards a common goal.

You are at home with your feelings, you are people-oriented and outstanding observers of people, great listeners and committed to making the world a better place. You prefer to learn by talking about experiences; listening and watching quietly, then responding to others and discussing ideas. You work well in groups or teams but also enjoy reading quietly.

You dislike confusion and conflict, environments where mistakes are openly criticised or where you cannot discuss their perceptions. You have a thinking style that puts perception before judgement, subjective knowledge before objective facts and reflection before action.

You prefer to make decisions based on feelings, and are experiential before conceptual.

For your Willpower Challenge, you will achieve great success if you work in a group or team. The support of others will keep you on track and you will enjoy the shared experience; but don't be brought down by others' failures – carve your own path if you have to.

Style 2 learners like to critique information and collect objective data. You are tough minded about gathering correct and precise answers. You thrive in environments where intellect is challenged and you like to demonstrate that you know your facts thoroughly.

You have a knowledge-oriented style; good at conceptualising material; analyse your experiences and organise ideas; you are highly organised and at home with details and data.

You prefer to learn through lectures and objective explanations, by working independently and systematically, and by reading.

You have a thinking style that is objective, reflecting before acting. You are often perceived as impersonal and conceptual rather than experiential. You tend to make judgements first, then support them with your perceptions.

For your *Willpower Challenge*, you will like to go it alone and research every aspect of your challenge. You will want to know everything you need to know and may well delay the start of your challenge as you want no surprises. Just get started.

Style 3 learners enjoy experimenting and testing ideas. You learn best by using problem solving to make sense of ideas. You quickly know when something is workable and succeed when straightforward thinking is needed and tasks are measurable.

You are drawn to how things work. You are at home with tasks and deadlines, are productive and committed to making the world work better, and you believe in your ability to get the job done. You prefer to learn through active problem solving; step-by-step procedures; manipulating and constructing; demonstrations; experimentation and tinkering; also competition.

You have a thinking style that is objective with facts over ideas, action before reflection, and judgement before perception. Your style is impersonal.

For your Willpower Challenge, you will be practical and organised and will no doubt already have a spreadsheet for tracking your challenge. You may have to read a little – not your favourite thing – to become expert in your challenge and to understand how others have been successful.

Style 4 learners prefer original thinking which involves trial and error problem solving. You enjoy situations that permit the exploration and application of ideas and the unconventional. You can tolerate the chaos of evolving ideas before the emergence of new possibilities.

You are proud of your subjectivity, at home with ambiguity and change, you can be great risk takers and entrepreneurs. You act to extend your experiences and to challenge boundaries for the sake of growth, and you believe in your ability to influence what happens. You initiate learning by looking for unique aspects of information and you sustain learning through trial and error.

You prefer to learn by self-discovery, talking, convincing others, looking for creative solutions to problems and engaging in free flights of ideas. You also like to work independently and tackle open-ended academic tasks with lots of options. Your interpersonal skills are good.

You have a thinking style that is perception first with little attention to judgement. You are subjective, action-oriented and more experiential than conceptual.

For your Willpower Challenge, you will want to start immediately and learn as you proceed. You may want to pause and explore previously successful methods and take time to think about feedback on progress.

Style 1 Learning Solution
An example of a successful Style 1 learning solution would be Alcoholics Anonymous. Let me introduce you to *Grace* and her story about overcoming her drinking problem. AA is a great example of support for a Style 1 learner.

> *"I had reached rock bottom, drinking a bottle of Vodka a night alone at home regularly. My laptop was open on the kitchen table and I clicked on Facebook and there was a friend of mine, Tracy, asking how I was. Tracy had a drink problem way back and I knew that she'd stopped drinking but I knew nothing about how. I hadn't seen*

her for 30 years and I thought for once, don't say I'm fine, be honest, and said, I'm really bad, I feel terrible. She came back and said, is it drinking? And for that split second I thought, what a cheek, her asking me if it's drinking. But I wrote, yes, it is. And she phoned me and told me about AA.

So she took me to Alcoholics Anonymous that day. I sat there and I looked at the bunch of people in the room and I thought I've got nothing in common with these people. Everyone is invited to share their thoughts for the day and it was only then that I identified with absolutely everybody in that room as they told their stories.

The harrowing stories of women losing their children really made a difference to my thinking. I was brought up in an alcoholic home and I just didn't want my son to have an alcoholic mother. I realised I wasn't there emotionally for him despite working from home. I had a degree in journalism, and yet everything that was important to me was now unimportant, I didn't have time for anything apart from drinking. After the meeting I sat down with him that night and watched TV and it was the first time that we'd sat and laughed for a long time. I went to that AA meeting every Monday after that. This was my ritual.

They say 90 days is the turning point. So you're supposed to do 90 meetings in 90 days. As soon as I'd decided not to drink I had the best sleep I've had in years. I woke ready for the day and for the rest of my life. Honesty and belief that you can do it if you put your mind to it, was the message from all there at that meeting. And of course AA is a fellowship which supports you throughout."

Style 2 Learning Solution
An Example of a Style 2 learning solution would be reading Allen Carr's Easy Way to Stop Smoking.

I first heard of this method to stop smoking when my friend Mary's partner bought her Allen Carr's book. He had issued an ultimatum that he wanted to marry her but not if she continued to smoke. She had been waiting for him to propose for years so she was very motivated, stopped smoking immediately after the last page and has never looked back. This is an example of Style 2 learning as Carr focuses on rational argument and his book is educational and inspirational. Page by page he confronts and destroys every reason a smoker has for smoking so that there is nowhere to go except give up. He also asserts it is easy, with few withdrawal symptoms and cravings to return to smoking. So powerful is his argument that one woman I talked to said that she has not completed the final chapter as she knows that she will have to give up smoking after that. Let's hope that she does.

His major points are:

- There is nothing beneficial about smoking. Inhaling smoke is a horrible experience which you only think you need because smoking is all about nicotine addiction.
- You are brainwashed into thinking that smoking is essential. Books or movies featuring last requests of the condemned man always include, yes, the smoking of the last cigarette. It's never a cup of coffee or a chocolate muffin! It inculcates the belief that smoking is a joyous prop for your ascent to heaven or hell with one last puff.
- Cigarettes create the void you try to fill with another cigarette. They hook you into a dependence belief with cigarette companies profiting from your addiction. It makes you miserable as you crave the next smoke.
- He also maintains that you don't need patches or vaping as those simply prolong your nicotine dependency. So just give up.
- It takes three weeks to get over the side effects of stopping, which are only of moderate severity and easily overcome.

The book seems to work as well as his courses and clinics as over a hundred thousand people have given up smoking as a result.

Style 3 Learning Solution

Style 3 learners are exceptional at monitoring their goals. They enjoy listing all that they require to do and love to produce a progress spreadsheet. Everything practical is thought about in advance.

Todd Whiteford provides a great example of Style 3 learning in his preparation for the Marathon des Sables:

> *"You need to be determined with lots of self-belief but much of the race is really a kind of management exercise with much attention to detail. We saw really super fit guys who just weren't prepared and they just crumbled in the desert. You can't just show up, put your shorts on and run; you need to have medical*

supplies, the right food and you need to have a bag that's not too heavy. We saw guys who were much fitter than us who on the first day failed because they hadn't prepared for the temperature, or their bags were too heavy, or they didn't have the right suit. So you have to have the analytical attention to preparation that an expedition leader would have."

Style 4 Learning Solution
Style 4 learners, on the other hand, are trial and error learners. They just like to jump in and do it.

I have personal experience of this style of learning solution. I was invited to sing in Wagner's *Die Meistersinger von Nürnberg* with Scottish Opera chorus. I had been in the audience the previous season so I knew the complexity of the music, especially in the fight scene with its 16-part harmony while fighting and running around the stage. This was going to be a Willpower Challenge of giant proportions.

Arthur Oldham, the chorus master, was quite exceptional and used unusual methods to get a chorus prepared. It was the first day of rehearsals and those of us who were new to *Die Meistersinger* were taken separately and had to sight read the score. Arthur then asked us to put aside the music and remember what we had sung. Yikes. Mistakes were acceptable, which was just as well as they were plentiful with hardly anything approximating "correct". I had never experienced this before – the freedom to get it wrong. We returned to our scores, then repeatedly put them aside, until by the end of the day we were remembering huge parts of the music. The preparation in between rehearsals was so much easier.

Of course, at some stage Arthur Oldham expected you to be word and note perfect. He had the terrifying habit of standing in front of you, touching your nose with his and defying you to get music and words wrong.

Wrestling, running, jumping and fighting while singing in 16-part harmony was easier than I thought because of his grounding. Arthur used a trial and error approach that certainly suited my Style 4 learning style, but possibly made others very uncomfortable. For me the freedom to make mistakes enabled me to memorise speedily and be free for whatever the director wanted me to do on stage. Arthur was a wonderful, innovative man who sadly is no longer with us.

My husband is a Style 3 learner. When on a weight loss programme his daily "weigh ins" are posted in a chart for his progress review, whereas I eat less and hope for the best. While writing this book he kept asking to see my prepared table of contents, and I kept replying that I am Mind Mapping the chapters as I go and the table of contents will emerge as a result. He would not be able to tolerate that approach. *Vive la difference!*

MOTIVATION

An important, if not crucial, part of willpower is knowing why you want to resist temptation or do something challenging.

For Grace it was wanting to stop drinking so that her son would not grow up with an alcoholic mother.

For my friend Mary it was to give up smoking so that she could marry Richard.

For Abby it was to get out of the house so that she could eventually go to university.

For Jamie it was showing himself that he can continue to face challenges as a quadruple amputee.

Being clear about why you are facing a Willpower Challenge helps you to maintain focus and, when things get tough, the why of it keeps you going.

Let's hear about why *Julie Ashmore* embarks on adventures. A business woman and mother of two children, she is one of only 200 people to ski to the South Pole.

"It was when I was turning 40 and having a midlife crisis. I felt that I was in danger of losing my identity. I was very happy with where I was heading from a career perspective and from a family perspective. I had my two amazing children and was a business woman with a great career, but I felt I was essentially losing who I was. I wanted to reconnect with all the things that I'd dreamt of doing in my 20s and be a person in my own right, and not just that mum, wife, partner, employee.

I was actually very ill as a child and I've reflected back and wondered why I am the way I am. I had epilepsy, so I was wrapped in metaphorical cotton wool by my parents and wasn't allowed to do as many things as I wanted to do – swimming for example. I was diagnosed at the age of 4 and discharged at 12. But those are important times in growth and development. I got into my late teens and 20s lacking in confidence, but I've now realised I am actually very strong and very resilient mentally."

A THEORY OF MOTIVATION

There are many theories about motivation, but one that impinges on willpower is intrinsic (internal) and extrinsic (external) motivation.

Intrinsic Motivation

Intrinsic motivation has been studied since the early 1970s by Robert White and later Susan Harter. Intrinsic motivation is the self-desire to seek out new things and new challenges, to analyse one's capacity, to observe and to gain knowledge. It is driven by an interest or enjoyment in the task itself, and exists within the individual rather than relying on external pressures or a desire for reward. The phenomenon of intrinsic motivation was first acknowledged within experimental studies of animal behaviour. In these studies, it was evident that even animals would engage in curiosity-driven behaviour in the absence of reward. For example, students who are intrinsically motivated are more likely to engage willingly as well as work to improve their skills – which will increase their capabilities – and are interested in mastering a topic, not just in achieving good grades.

Intrinsic motivation can be long-lasting and self-sustaining. Efforts to build this kind of motivation are also typically efforts at promoting student learning. Such efforts often focus on the subject rather than rewards or punishments.

Extrinsic Motivation

Extrinsic motivation refers to the performance of an activity in order to attain a desired outcome and it is the opposite of intrinsic motivation. Extrinsic motivation comes from influences outside the individual. Usually it is used to attain outcomes that a person wouldn't get from intrinsic motivation. Common extrinsic motivations are rewards (for example money or grades) for showing the desired behaviour, and the threat of punishment following misbehaviour. Competition is an extrinsic motivator because it encourages the performer to win and beat others, not simply to enjoy the intrinsic rewards of the activity. A cheering crowd and the desire to win a trophy would also be extrinsic incentives.

Teresa Amabile in her book *The Progress Principle* discovered when reviewing the daily diaries of 200 employees from 7 companies that if people are intrinsically motivated – they love their work – it is counterproductive to try to reward them extrinsically. They were insulted when they were offered a bonus. What did make a difference was being given feedback from a boss for a job well done. However, another study showed that school children who were rewarded with a book showed more reading behaviour in the future, suggesting that some rewards do not undermine intrinsic motivation (if, of course, the kids really love reading – which they may not).

It would be advantageous if you are intrinsically motivated to complete a Willpower Challenge, but the reality is that you might not. If your challenge involves resisting the temptation of smoking, gambling, drinking alcohol, eating certain foods or trading your seat in front of the television for running in inclement weather, you may not be experiencing the joy of the intrinsic motivation journey . . . or at least not yet.

Willpower is the initial grit that gets us over the temptation to return to the status quo or our default setting of doing nothing in the face of a demanding challenge. I have written elsewhere that it takes three weeks to establish a new behaviour, and on average another nine weeks of repeating that new behaviour to turn it into a habit. During the willpower stage extrinsic motivators can be very helpful. These can take many forms. For me it was to travel to a warm place, Lanzarote, to write *Willpower*. I would be away from distraction, focused . . . and warm.

Willpower Motivators
- Monitor your progress: success is its own reward.
- Play music while working late on a project.
- Watch television while ironing, sewing, repairing.
- Get feedback from friends about your progress.
- Travel to sunnier climes to write a book!

Get your dopamine where you can, but don't just reward yourself with what tempts you! During three weeks of grit and determination and using extrinsic rewards to keep going, you will gradually feel better about your new behaviour. After this, as you repeat this new behaviour and gain mastery, you are more likely to become intrinsically motivated. You will enjoy your new behaviour as an end in itself. Hear more about this in Part Three.

Allen Carr talks in his book about getting through three weeks of withdrawal from smoking then feeling glorious freedom from the tyranny of nicotine.

Grace talks about the twelve-week AA philosophy of "one day at a time". Now she is comfortable eschewing alcohol and will happily go to a bar with friends, and enjoy observing them becoming befuddled as she remains sober.

When I was a student at Glasgow University there was always coffee, hot water and milk in the common room, but never any sugar. I started carrying around small packets of sugar or sweeteners in my handbag, which eventually led to a gooey mess. No self-respecting woman wants a sticky handbag, so I decided to give up sugar in coffee.

It took three weeks of refusing sugar in the common room (which wasn't difficult – there was none on offer) to going cold turkey at home and in coffee shops. For three weeks my enjoyment of coffee plummeted, but after three weeks it became easier. Then, after nine weeks of repetition, a friend mistakenly added some sugar to my coffee and despite catching her mid-spoonful a few grains entered my cup. I spat out my coffee. I was sugar free. Just to make sure this wasn't a fluke I suggested my mother went through the three-week process too. She left sugar out of coffee for three weeks plus another nine and never looked back.

This 12-week rule will be discussed further in Part Three: New Habits for Old.

REMEMBER YOUR GOALS

Another factor in deviating from our goals is that we forget them. There are many ways to overcome this and I have outlined some below.

- Write your goals down and place the list somewhere in your sight line every day. Put them on a computer screen saver, on a fridge, in a drawer at work, at the front of a diary.
- Draw your goals. Drawing triggers memory like no other tool. If you are resistant to that idea, cut out some relevant pictures for

magazines. We remember the visual image 30% more than the written word.

· Get people around you to remind you and reward you for progress.

Reminders in the Digital Era

I took part in a BBC Radio programme about willpower with Maneesh Sethi, creator of the Pavlok, a reminder wristband device which provides a reminder shock to your wrist. He told us about a Willpower Challenge he had with Facebook a few years ago – he actually hired a girl to slap him in the face whenever he used Facebook. He had become aware he was wasting too much time on a daily basis on social media but seemed powerless to stop. The slap worked and his productivity increased by four times. He knew he was on to something interesting and created a device that would work in areas where willpower is a challenge.

The result is the Pavlok, a wristband that sends you an electric shock every time you go into your overdraft, or you go over a pre-determined limit. Partnering with CEO David Webber from Intelligent Environments he says that it is all about giving customers the choice to control how they spend money. You could get a shock while paying for products. If you don't fancy getting a zap whenever you overspend, you can choose to have your heating turned down by a recommended three degrees instead. This isn't to punish you but turning down your heating could save you £255 a year, according to Intelligent Environments. The temperature control system works using Google's smart thermostat system and I suppose saves you from being shocked.

No bank has announced it will use the system just yet, but Intelligent Environments has reassured potential customers their information will be safe.

The Pavlok also helps people to stop smoking by giving them a zap: so if your Willpower Challenge is to give up smoking, it might be time to get this wristband – which can give you an electric shock every time you reach for a fag. The shock is pretty mild, but users claim it creates a reminder and an association which makes it easy to stop smoking.

You can also use the thing to give up sugar, and even Facebook – using the paired app to zap yourself whenever you lapse. You can also hand the control to friends, so they zap you instead. Perhaps a bridge too far.

The device is on sale now via Amazon, and already has a lot of scarily enthusiastic testimonials from people who've electric-shocked their way to inner peace. They can be triggered by sensors, a remote control or a manual tap.

Visualising Success

Visualisation is a powerful tool and I was brought up on the idea of visualising success at the end point of a goal, but now research has found that a more effective way of visualising the future is to think about the processes or steps that are involved in reaching a goal rather than just the end-state of achieving it.

Outcome and process have been tested experimentally by a couple of researchers, Pham and Taylor, who had students either visualise their ultimate goal of doing well in an exam or the steps they would take to reach that goal – i.e. their studying regime. The results were clear-cut. Participants who visualised themselves reading and gaining the required skills and knowledge, spent longer actually studying and got better grades in the exam.

There were two reasons that visualising the process rather than the outcome worked:

Planning Visualising the process helped focus attention on the steps needed to reach the goal, so planning and control were increased.

Emotion Visualising the process led to reduced anxiety.

So setting mini goals and visualising mini goals works.

Turly Humphries, founder of Circle Sports which helps young people into employment, has used visualisation to great effect.

> *"My big vision is to create a chain of shops that will give work experience to young people looking for employment. There's no such thing as social buying really, but I am really impressed by the social conscience of young people who contact us wanting to help and do internships.*
>
> *I want to do it without stigmatising the young people, in an environment where they feel comfortable with. I want us to be separate from the job centre because that's a negative association.*
>
> *I react to big challenges in my life by visualising the other side. I have previously visualised a new shop and put myself in the picture.*

I visualised getting the keys, going into the shop, walking around the space, setting it all up, and it really worked. I thought it was all non-sense, but actually visualising really worked. I am now in the shop I visualised."

Neil Fachie, Gold medal Paralympian and a World Record holding cyclist, also talks about the power of visualisation to win.

"It's hard not to start thinking too much when you're getting closer to a race. Whenever I'm getting too nervous, I try and visualise the race. I think of the processes involved, rather than what the outcome is going to be and what that'll mean.

It's amazing, actually, when you do visualise a race your heart rate starts to mimic what it would be during the race, that sort of excite-ment and adrenaline kicks in as you picture phases of the race. I think it's something that's really important, particularly at the start of a cycling event when it is very technical. Visualising the processes I think really helps, so that when you come to do it, it becomes almost automatic.

If you imagine something you do every day in life and you imagine doing it over and over again, the chances are you'll do it as you imagined because it's second nature. It can be quite calming as well. If you visualise it and you're good at visualising and you're not visualising it going wrong, then you become confident and I find it calming."

Visualisation Exercise
So, return to your page of goals and mini goals and memorise the steps and then close your eyes.

Visualisation builds a bridge between you and the future and allows you to think and feel positively about the achievement of your goals in advance and the steps you need to take to get there. To practise visualisa-tion, you first need to relax.

Relaxation and Visualisation
- Sit on a comfortable seat or lie down on a bed or floor, supporting your head with a cushion.
- Take a deep breath and exhale slowly.
- Do this again.

- Tense and relax your arms and hands.
- Bring your shoulders towards your ears and then relax.
- Bring your chin to your chest, stretching the back of your neck, then relax.
- Tense every muscle in your face; forehead, eyes, nose, and clench your teeth.
- Take a deep breath and tense your stomach muscles as if preparing for a blow to that area, then relax.
- Tense your thigh muscles and then relax.
- Stretch the back of your legs and turn your feet up towards your face, then relax.
- As you breathe out, let your body become heavier and heavier, more and more relaxed.

When you are relaxed, in your mind's eye imagine you are the star in your own movie. Visualise yourself as vividly as possible. Turn the brightness controls up on the imaginary screen to achieve more definition and colour in your vision.

First, imagine the old you, with all that you would like to change, doing all the things you would be doing as the old you.

- What would you be saying?
- How would you be acting?
- What would you be worrying about?

Visualise these things for 30 seconds then put a dull frame around this picture of the old you and move that to the right until it's gone.

Now erect a new movie screen. You are looking at the *new you* – see yourself achieving each of the *mini goals* towards your Willpower Challenge. Visualise the steps now. What would you be doing, who would you be with, what would you be wearing, how would you be looking, how would you be feeling? Place some adjectives beside this image of the new you; for example, happy, relaxed, successful, confident. Add whatever adjectives you desire into your vision.

See this movie image enlarge itself and move off towards the horizon. Visualise the new you going toward the future, reaching each mini goal as you progress, and tell yourself "This is how it will be". Place a realistic date beside this vision and tell yourself it will happen.

Repeat this exercise every night before going to sleep. Success will be yours when you take the steps to get there.

Click on the link www.rostaylorcompany.com/relaxation to hear four different types of relaxation exercise: the first two focus on muscle relaxation, the latter two on visualisation. You will receive an email with the link. Copy to your phone or tablet.

INSPIRING YOU TOWARD YOUR WILLPOWER CHALLENGE

Here are some final words from *Julie Ashmore* to inspire you towards your Willpower Challenge:

> *"For the South Pole 22-day trek not only did I have to train by walking, cycling and running, but I also had to do some specialist training which actually involved pulling a tyre, well three tyres, around my local village green – which was quite funny. It's specialist because there are certain core muscles that you need to build and develop to be able to pull your sled with all your gear and the only way to develop those muscles is pulling tyres. So to begin with I was doing it at night in darkness because I was embarrassed in case people saw me and thought I'd lost my marbles, and then I realised that this was just becoming really inconvenient so I started being brave and doing it on a Sunday afternoon.*
>
> *I also had to camp out in a freezer with the team of three guys. The freezer was a 40-foot container with one door and no windows with a temperature of -25 C. Imagine us in a pitched tent inside a freezer for the weekend.*
>
> *If I don't do the training, the actual event is going to hurt even more and that motivates me to find the time – but it's not easy with children and work. So there are times when I've had to juggle and I've found myself combining the children with my training. But the preparation time is essential.*
>
> *The whole trek was much more severe than I'd expected, even though I'd read up a lot on it, you don't know what it feels like until you get there. And it was also more draining emotionally than physically, although physically it was hard. I was pulling a very heavy sled and doing that for 10 hours at a time was draining. But emotionally it was even more draining. I was very isolated. At the South Pole, the wind is in your face and you can't expose any skin, or you'd get burnt and get frostbite, I hadn't appreciated that because you're all covered up you can't actually talk to anybody. And I found that very*

hard because I'm somebody that likes to be around people, I like to be in a team. I took an iPod but it kept freezing up so that didn't work either so it was literally me, with my pain of pulling my sled for all of those hours a day. And also there's nothing visually stimulating, it's just flat with white ice. So it's just you and your thoughts. I found it really hard to keep going but keep going I did.

When I reached the South Pole, it was the centenary anniversary of the explorer Scott, so there was a cricket match happening the next day. I got caught up in that and realised not only was I in such an amazing place but I was one of only 200 people who were there and that was really when the sense of achievement and pride started to come through. I played in that celebratory cricket match and won."

Actions for Willpower
- Plan your preparation time for a Challenge. Without it you could become unstuck if it's a *Julie* kind of challenge.
- Know your learning style so that you choose the mode of your challenge carefully. You will be more motivated throughout.
- Julie is a Style 1 learner, so for her next challenge she will ensure she has team support to avoid the isolation she felt in her South Pole bid.
- The challenge may be uncomfortable, but the joy at the end is worth the pain.

REMINDERS

- Choose your goal or goals for your Willpower Challenge. These should be meaningful to you and worthwhile.
- Create mini goals for each of your goals. Starting small, succeeding, then building on that is motivational.
- Plan to fail so that you know in advance when you are likely to be vulnerable to temptation or backsliding and have a plan in place.
- Understand your learning style so that the learning solution for your challenge is suitable for you and sustains you.
- Keep reminders of your goals and mini goals around you prominently displayed as you might tend to forget them in the hurly burly of your life.
- Use some extrinsic motivation to reward you, especially in the initial stages of your challenge.

- Create a mantra to keep you focused.
- New circumstances or physical challenges can be uncomfortable. This will pass and the fulfilment of achievement will be worth it.
- Relax and visualise the steps to success.
- Congratulations. You have your goals and mini goals in place for your Willpower Challenge and a plan to go forward. Part Three will take you on a journey to embed your new behaviour so that it becomes part of who you are.

PART THREE
New Habits for Old

Willpower is especially important for that first incursion into your goal or new behaviour. Once that new behaviour is established, turning it into a habit with repetition will embed it. Chris, one of the young men we interviewed at Canal College, when asked about his willpower said: "I have so much willpower I have stopped smoking four times." Not quite willpower as we know it!

This part of the book aims to put an end to trying and failing continuously and to embed new behaviour with willpower. We are going to look at the links between willpower and habit and thus how to achieve the good habits you have always desired. It is crucial to the success of your Willpower Challenge that you understand the nature of habit formation.

Here is a scamper through past and present philosophical and psychological thinking on the subject of rational thinking and habit.

Greek philosophy was about the rationality of man and it was Plato's belief that it was our thinking and ideas that created human reality. Freud reinforced this concept with his rational "ego" overcoming the unruly instinctual "id" for good mental health. However, psychologist William James in 1890 claimed that we were really a mass of instincts, impulses and emotions and not entirely the higher-order beings that Plato and Freud postulated. He was the first theorist to believe that our instincts – with associated automatic thoughts – were quick ways of responding to life around us rather than the slower method of ponderously thinking everything through. Aaron Beck, in turn, took these ideas forward to create Cognitive Behavioural Psychology. It is this speedy thinking and responding which can be a life saver on threatening occasions but is also the underpinning of habit formation.

Experiments have now revealed that habits rule much of our life: about 50% give or take. MIT research in 1990 on maze-learning in rats discovered that as each rat learned their way around the maze, their mental activity in the cerebral cortex decreased until within a week it went quiet. What was happening? The rats' maze-learning habits became automatic so that they required very little mental processing – similarly for us humans. Our brains are constantly looking for ways to save effort on basic behaviours so that we can concentrate on higher-order things like major decisions and problem solving. Obama has a wardrobe of grey suits so that he doesn't have to make too many decisions in the morning, and Mark Zuckerberg has mountains of grey t shirts for a similar reason. (Is there something about grey that I've missed?)

The downside of this habit-forming process is that our brains don't discriminate between good and bad habits. Unless you use the deliberation of willpower to fight a habit, a well-used routine will happen automatically without any conscious thought. And these habits can be remarkably persevering over time. There were early psychological experiments carried out on pigeons who were rewarded with pellets of food if they pressed a lever. The experimenters stopped delivering the food pellets to see how the pigeons would respond. These poor birds kept pressing that lever even when the food pellets had been absent for a very long time. So, even without reward, the pigeon's habitual lever-pressing behaviour still persisted.

Habits are stored in the midbrain, particularly in the basal ganglia. As activity in the basal ganglia increases, so activity in the prefrontal cortex decreases. Habits are very important as we would be overcome with detail if we had to think about everything we do every day, so it was a glorious plus in the evolutionary process that we kept that lower brain while our higher-order cerebral cortex was developing.

Habits are formed early in our lives. The first three years are crucial in this process, as we learn from our parents or parent figures. We may not have a conscious memory of this process, but believe me it happened and the habits are there. We are like our parents, perhaps not in the context of our lives – you are perhaps a lawyer while your parents were retailers – but in terms of how you interact with the world.

Wanting to discover more about the impact of early years, I interviewed Graham Allen Member of Parliament for Nottingham North. He leads a cross party committee for Early Intervention to help children and parents from disadvantaged backgrounds.

ORIGINS OF WILLPOWER WITH GRAHAM ALLEN

"If a baby, child or young person has social and emotional capability, then they have willpower, resilience, the ability to learn and to be a social animal: all those things are facilitated if you've got that bedrock from your parents.

This comes from having positive childhood experiences with good parenting, especially a positive relationship between mother and child. A baby is hardwired to give you cues to stimulate it. That's why they are the shape they are and have the eyes they have, the sounds they make. It's a sort of ruthless ability to manipulate the older being who is giving them the care, and that produces a virtuous circle. The reason: the preservation of the species, and the ability to reproduce. It means a baby is beginning a training course to be the good parent of tomorrow. It is cyclical. The reason I underline this is that if you have bad experiences, you will repeat the bad things in the same way as when you have positive experiences you will repeat the good things. It all traces back.

The Californian Felitti has researched Adverse Childhood Experience and the long-term effects. He created a list of these experiences and if you've got 3 out of 12 then you're regarded as having an adverse childhood and the more boxes you ticked, the more discernible is the impact on your mental health, your ability to make lasting relationships and your willpower. It also affects physical wellbeing. So in a target group of 40 to 50-year-old Americans, there was a high incidence of diabetes, stroke and heart attack, discernibly higher than the national average of a population who didn't have adverse childhood experiences.

It's all about fight or flight. When babies and young children are in a constant state of anxiety in an abusive home the subsequent release of cortisol has a scouring impact on the brain and doesn't allow them to have a measured response to stimuli. People grow up with a hair trigger response rather than the ability to respond in a more rational way to conflicts around them. An example – 'I'm not going to punch you because you are looking at me strangely'. But if I don't have the ability to stop myself doing that, I don't have willpower. Abuse is denying will in people and it's removing their ability to respond rationally. The government's

Early Intervention work is focused on babies up to the age of three and targets parents from disadvantaged backgrounds, providing support to avert the long-term effects of abusive and disadvantaged homes."

Despite coming from disadvantaged backgrounds, people can change that "hair trigger response" and learn the cool system of willpower.

Psychiatrist *Eric Berne* describes this cyclical learning process in his theory of *Transactional Analysis*. He proposed the concept that all experiences were laid down on a "tape" during our early years to be accessed later when necessary. Although we can't remember the first three years of our lives, that tape was still playing and is playing to this day. So Berne has it that there are three aspects to our attitudes and behaviour: the Parent, the Child and the Adult. He calls these aspects "egos" (see Figure 3.1).

The *Parent ego* has two sides: the critical, disciplining, restricting parent and the helpful, caring, loving parent. The controlling parent is the one who scolds when the children are late for dinner and the caring parent is the one who is happy they arrived home safely.

So your parents are, in his theory, huge influencers in your lives. The basic information that you use comes from a lifetime of experience with parents and teachers, particularly in early life. Remarks like "Sit up straight at the table", "Use your knife and fork not your fingers", "Bring it here, Mummy will help you", will be on your parent tape whether you like it or not and can be played back at any time.

You can hear children scolding each other like parents, for example "Don't touch that – Mummy says so". When we feel, think, talk and behave in the way we remember our parents doing, then we are playing our parent tape. Often it is the parent's attitude which shows in later life, rather than the actual words, e.g. "Do it the way I tell you please . . . " or "Leave it up to me, I'll do it".

The Parent ego is very strongly imprinted on the brain and works automatically, particularly if you are criticised. The critical parent uses words and phrases like: "right and wrong", "good and bad", "what will people say", "you must never", "stop that at once", "that's the limit!" The helpful or caring parent uses words and phrases like "Oh dear! What a shame", "Don't be afraid", "Take care", "I'll help you", "Don't be late", "It won't take me long to . . . ".

Now, while we are soaking up all this parental influence, we are indulging in being children and a child tape is playing. The child tape has recorded all your emotions, all your early experiences, together with your initial views of yourself and others. The *Child ego* reacts emotionally with the feelings and instincts of childhood.

There are two facets of child behaviour. The natural child who is primitive, impulsive, instinctive, undisciplined and demanding, and the adapted child who "does as it is told", is polite, sometimes manipulative, and gives rise to guilt, rebellion, obedience and compromises.

Examples of phrases used by the Child ego are "Let's play", "I won't", "it's mine", "I will in a minute", "Wow!", "Let's not be serious, let's party".

There is a third ego in the Berne theory: the Adult.

The *Adult ego* is the mature and deliberating part of your personality. Your actions and words, when this tape is played, are sensible and well-considered, as opposed to the almost automatic reactions of the Parent and Child egos. The Adult ego collects information, evaluates it, works out probabilities, tackles and solves problems, all in an original, calm collected way. You concentrate on facts, not feelings and prejudices. The Adult ego is independent of age. As a rule, the Adult ego asks questions and seeks out facts, for example "What is that?", "Let's find out", "What do you think?", "Let's experiment", "Why did that happen?", "Let's define it", "What are the choices?", "How can we handle it best?".

Early habits are long lasting and, unless reviewed and changed, will persist throughout our lives, even into the following generations if you have children. This early learning may propel you positively through life, but it might just as easily contain limiting beliefs and habits that you need to change in order to reach your goals.

I was asked by a local GP to see Maria, a pregnant young woman who suffered from anxiety, to help her to relax because she couldn't be prescribed any medication. I quickly came to realise that her anxiety was all about her mother who lived in the upper flat of the family home. She was an outspoken and controlling woman who constantly entered her daughter's house with no warning and would turn up to friends' dinners uninvited and take over the conversation. Sadly, her daughter had allowed this to happen and was habitually passive towards her mother's increasingly overpowering behaviour. She had been brought up to be "nice" and had learned her habit of capitulating behaviour directly and

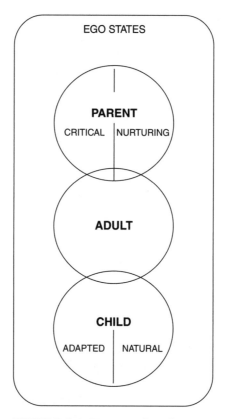

FIGURE 3.1 Transactional
Analysis – Ego States

early on from her father who had done anything for a quiet life. He had died five years previously so she was now the focus of her mother's attention. Maria and her husband wanted to move house before the baby's arrival – well you would, wouldn't you – but her mother was incensed by the idea. Anytime they viewed houses and focused on a favourite, her mother would have a "turn"– an unspecified fainting episode.

EGO STATES

So what to do about Maria and her mother?

I suggested to Maria that she check out the nature of the "turns" with her doctor and, as suspected, no underlying medical reason had been discovered after many extensive investigations. We then practised how she could assert herself with her mother. In advance of dinner parties, her mother was asked to supper the night before so that she would feel included not neglected, but was then informed that she wasn't invited the following evening. Maria had a great phrase she used: "Mum you know how you love to talk, well it inhibits others so we would rather you didn't attend this one." Tears and imprecations ensued, but both she and her husband worked hard at remaining unmoved. Then they made an offer on a house and as predicted it was accompanied by a fainting episode from her mother. Maria was supportive but continued with the house purchase. They sold the family home and bought a bungalow for her mother nearby . . . but not too near. Maria's anxiety disappeared and her little girl is now learning the habits of an assertive mother without realising it.

Let's now look at how habits are formed and what you can do to change bad ones to good, as well as how long it might take for that process to happen. Psychologists have posited a three-step model of habit formation (see Figure 3.2).

The cue or stimulus triggers a behaviour or routine which is rewarded, and with enough repetition this cycle becomes automatic. For a rat it might be sitting in front of a maze, running through it the right way and being rewarded by a piece of cheese at the end; for a pigeon learning to press a lever for the reward of a food pellet. A human example might be poor Maria's father who, with the stimulus of an angry wife, would say nothing to gain the reward of a quiet life. And Maria learned the same strategy, so her mother's behaviour continued and strengthened over

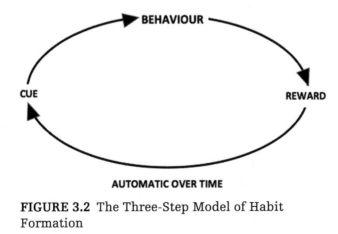

FIGURE 3.2 The Three-Step Model of Habit Formation

time. The piece in the habit cycle that had to change was her response to her mother – as well as realising that her mother was not going to reward her for making these changes.

And there's the rub. When you are embarking on habit change it doesn't happen automatically just because you decide on it. We know that habits are formed in the midbrain, in the basal ganglia, so conscious thought will not be sufficient to reverse them. There are skills involved, like self-awareness of why the passive behaviour is there in the first place and assertiveness to be learned so that you can move forward. Also, reward might not be immediate but long term. So retraining the midbrain is a Willpower Challenge.

THE WILLPOWER STAGE OF HABIT FORMATION

The question asked by everyone embarking on a willpower project is: how long will all this willpower and habit formation take? To answer this, the research must be reviewed.

It all goes back to a plastic surgeon, Maxwell Maltz, who noticed that when he performed operations on his patients, it took them about three weeks to get used to seeing their new face. Similarly, when he performed amputations, patients would sense a phantom limb for about three weeks afterwards. He also noticed that when he tried to form new habits himself, it took him three weeks. He recounted this in his book *Psych-Cybernetics* in 1960.

More recently, in 2010, University College, London, conducted a study aimed at getting to the bottom of the question of how long it really takes us to develop a new habit. The study tracked 96 people over 12 weeks as they attempted to make a daily habit change: each participant chose a behaviour – like drinking a glass of water three times a day – then they had to recount how automatic the activity felt each time they did it. The researchers found that it took, on average, 66 days until the behaviour became automatic.

However, there was a lot of variation within each result as, for example, it took one person only 18 days to achieve an automatic habit, while another didn't get there at all by the end of the 84 days. Some behaviours appeared to become habitual more easily than others; for example, drinking a glass of water became a habit more quickly than doing 50 push-ups daily.

There has been much debate about the three-week habit rule. In my experience as a psychologist, firstly as a clinician then as an executive

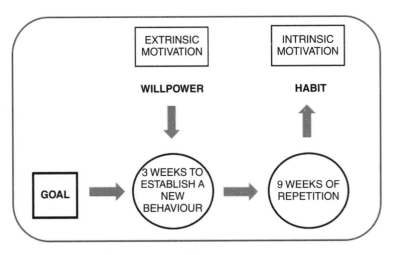

FIGURE 3.3 Willpower to Habit

coach, it takes on average three weeks to establish a new behaviour and another nine weeks of repetition of that new behaviour, give or take a week, to turn it into a habit. During that process there is the likelihood of extrinsic motivation, rewards of many sorts, being replaced by intrinsic motivation, a desire to complete a task for its own sake (see Figure 3.3).

The Stages of Habit Formation

1. *Weeks 1 to 3: Start the new behaviour.* If it is running half a mile every morning, then that pattern will have to be established. Alarms may have to be set earlier, the snooze button disabled, the weather ignored, kit washed and ready for wearing. Just getting out of bed requires willpower on a winter day. External rewards can be useful at this stage to motivate you, so plan them in advance. For example, run with a friend who calls at the house, have a celebration at the end of the three week mark to have something to aim for, or reward yourself with a new piece of kit.

2. *Weeks 4 to 6: Keep moving forward.* This mid-point is often the hardest, so don't let yourself start slacking now. Reminders of why you are doing this – keeping fit, losing weight – will help you keep moving towards your goal. Sometimes, just when you think you have really got into the rhythm of a new habit, there is a return of old behaviour called an "extinction burst" that kicks in. If this happens, get back on track. This is the point where willpower is required.

3. *Weeks 6 to 9*: Repetition is turning your running into a habit. At this point you are in the groove of your habit. Repetition up to nine weeks and beyond means that running every morning has become an automatic, habitual response. Daily running also should have become an end in itself, which means you are intrinsically motivated because you have experienced the rewarding results of your actions. Fitter, healthier, increased alertness at work, better decision making, sleeping more soundly and being much more relaxed. A whole clutch of good things.

So, in the big scheme of things, three weeks of willpower to establish a new behaviour, with another nine weeks of repetition, isn't bad if you have been a couch potato all your life.

Some habits can be established more speedily if they are simple actions, like my three weeks of no sugar in coffee. After that I couldn't bear a grain of sugar, never mind a spoonful. If it is a more complex set of behaviours – like getting up early, ready for a morning run in inclement weather – then it might take a little longer to establish.

One of my Willpower Challenges was to swim every day while writing *Willpower* in Lanzarote. It sounds as if it might be more reward than challenge but, believe me, the water in the local pool was extremely cold and uninviting. During the first three days my limbs became numb with the frigid temperatures, but by the end of the first week I was swimming more easily and at the end of three weeks I had increased my speed and number of lengths of the pool. I only missed two days when there were thunderstorms and I felt that a pool was not the place to be if lightning struck. So swimming towards the end of three weeks was becoming habitual with repetition; however, I hadn't planned in advance what to do when returning home. The proximity of the pool abroad made daily swimming easy, whereas at home it is further away requiring transport. The result: not swimming every day. Three weeks was enough to establish my new swimming behaviour, but the interruption stopped habit formation and extinction took place.

THE EXTINCTION BURST

When a habit disappears this is called extinction, but our old habits after three weeks are waiting in the wings to return if willpower fails. For example, you want to give up chocolate as part of a diet. You succeed in not buying any at the supermarket to stop temptation and all is going well for three weeks. You are in a meeting at work and in the centre of the table are a bowl of chocolates. Everyone has taken one and, after staring at the bowl, you have one in your mouth before you notice. No time to pause and plan, your prefrontal cortex overthrown, you are in the midst of an extinction burst when you might not only eat all the remaining chocolates in the dish but also buy the three-for-two offer on bags of sweets on the way home.

When the familiar cue of chocolate is presented to you, and in the disinhibiting company of others, it is easy to transgress and then make that an excuse to transgress even further. This is a blast of defiance from old habits stored in the basal ganglia and a very common part of the extinction process. This isn't a return to old ways – just your brain trying to find a way round your new "absence of chocolate behaviour". To give in to a return of your chocolate eating will lengthen the habit forming process the next time you try. Your brain now knows you gave in and will produce more cravings designed to undermine you in the future.

Most parents of young children will have experienced extinction bursts. A favourite childhood habit parents complain about is children not sleeping in their own beds. I was talking to a young couple a few weeks ago about Marcus, aged 3, who would not sleep in his own bed, or would sleep for three hours and then scream to be lifted into the parental bed just as they were falling asleep. As the husband said, it was easier just to let him get in as then he could go back to sleep, rather than get up and return him and be awake afterwards for hours. The trouble is, not returning him to his own bed allows the habit to continue. So for all you sleep-deprived parents, this is what to do:

Actions for Willpower: Parents of Young Children
1. Choose a week that is not too busy or stressful – well, less stressful anyway. Illness, overwork, arrival of a new baby would not be right times, perhaps.
2. Prepare your child for the change. Mention that its "sleep in your own bed week". Create drawings together about the new regime.
3. When your child comes into the parental bed, remain neutral emotionally – no hugs or kisses (that would be rewarding the old habit) and calmly return them to bed.

4. If they still don't like being left on their own, take a blanket and sleep on the floor beside them, not in the bed – unless you want to start that as a new habit – then return to bed when they fall asleep. And keep doing that. It is a bit of upfront investment for eventual payoff.

5. Just when you think you may have got this licked, and your child has been sleeping in their own bed for three consecutive nights, there they are at the side of your bed crying, begging to be let into yours. The screams get louder as you try to pick them up to return them. Your child is fighting, kicking so much you are beginning to believe that something is seriously wrong. You think "well perhaps just this once to calm him down". DO NOT DO IT. What you are witnessing is an extinction burst. Your child is trying every trick in the "three year old monster" behaviour book designed to get you to capitulate. If you do, you will have to start all over again and this time your child will know that if they escalate their bad behaviour, you will capitulate and give them what they want.

6. Reward your child with a small surprise in the morning for sleeping through the night in their own bed: a small game or toy and, of course, parental congratulations.

Consistency, Consistency, Consistency

I've heard parents claim this method has worked in three nights, others three weeks, but not giving in and being consistent are vital to success. Many mothers find it especially hard as they are programmed to respond to a crying child. They may even have formed that into a philosophy of child rearing, but if parents want to be two in a bed not three then follow the rules.

So consistency is vital in the formation of new habits. And of course willpower to remain steadfast in the face of extinction bursts, which are the last-ditch efforts of the lower brain to restore the old habit.

Replacement Aids Extinction: New for Old Works

Habits lurk. They are waiting to return. So when you are giving something up, there is evidence to show that if you replace the old habit with another more desirable one at the same time, then this helps to extinguish the old habit. So if you had a bag of nuts or a piece of fruit with you, then you might have been very much less persuaded by the chocolates in front of you on the table. This advanced planning for willpower glitches in the early days of habit formation increases the chance of success.

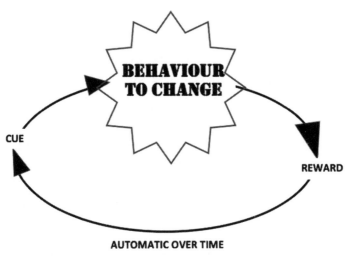

FIGURE 3.4 Our Response: We Can Change

Returning to our habit model, the cue remains the same – the desire for a snack – and the reward of satisfaction doesn't change; but our response, the behaviour in between, is up for grabs (see Figure 3.4).

Actions for Willpower: Behaviour Replacements

- If you crave a sandwich, eat a salad instead and make it easy for yourself. So go to a salad shop, not one that offers tempting sandwiches.
- If you love a sugary cereal in the morning, replace it with a non-sugar fruit and fibre alternative. Make sure all sugary cereals are unavailable in your house and off the shopping list. If you know where they are, in a weak moment – take it from me – you will indulge.
- When you desire a donut with your morning coffee, replace it with a piece of fruit. You might like to suggest to those around you that fruit replacement is the way to go too so you have their support and no enticing donuts.
- If you are a critical person, always looking for faults in others, then replace that behaviour by looking for the good and rewarding it consistently when you see it.
- Replace worry with relaxation. Learn the skills and practise every day. Spot the triggers for worry: the "oh dear what if it all goes wrong" and replace it with "well, so what!"
- If you are stubborn, digging your heels in when any change is suggested, become flexible. Look for the positives in every suggestion

and learn to say "how interesting". This commits you to nothing and lets you keep an open mind.

The trick is to make the new habit easy to acquire and the old one more difficult to re-emerge. As stated above, stop buying the food you want to avoid, have alternatives close to hand and on display. Ask those around you for support. I am so tempted socially to eat, drink and be merry, whereas I will happily keep to a diet regime on my own. We are who we hang out with. Review your friends. Are they who you want to be? Surround yourself with like-minded people.

If you want to stop being critical of others, then avoid the coffee time gossips who ritually destroy those around them during every break. When you want to be more flexible and positive, fraternise with those who are optimistic.

> **Reminder: it bears repeating!**
> A new behaviour takes three weeks to form plus another nine to become a habit.

MINI AND MULTIPLE HABITS

It is a common belief that it is good to focus on one behaviour change at a time so that you don't experience willpower depletion. I know as a young psychologist I had my patients list all the things they had to change after their first session with me. I was referred some very challenging people with complex lives and even more complex symptoms, so their lists were long. In those days I had the most unrealistic expectation that they would leave the session with me and start working on all the changes immediately. Imagine my surprise when they didn't return for a second session. So I learned not to overwhelm them with change and suggested instead that they focus on either the most pressing of behaviours to change or the ones that would make the most difference; however, I never suggested that they should tackle issues one at a time. That would take too long and some habits are easier to change than others and can be clustered.

We have so many habits and most of them are small. Can you think of any small habits you might have – such as biting your nails, twirling your hair, stroking your beard, etc. – that you've accidentally formed? There are hundreds of small habits you won't be aware of unless someone mentions them or they become problematic.

One ingredient of success is making the behaviours mini-sized, or "too small to fail". Pavlov, by rewarding a pigeon for making small moves to the right, ended up with a twirling pigeon. We are not dissimilar. Small habits aren't just possible, they're far more common than the major habits we tend to focus on (an exercise programme, stopping smoking, getting up early each morning, eating healthy food, etc.)

Neural pathways in the brain are the engines of habits.

- A neuron fires down a pathway in your brain. I have heard it described as like a "machete carving its way through a jungle of dendrites". This is the cue part of habit.
- You then perform a *behaviour* or routine.
- You get positive feedback or a *reward* for the behaviour.
- That neural pathway is strengthened into a habit with repetition over time.

Each time this happens, it leads to a very small amount of strengthening, but when you add it up over weeks and months, it's meaningful. Gradually strengthening habits is an excellent example of how, for example, exercise works over time.

It's actually very unusual for the brain to make large changes. It's not built to change quickly, either, which makes it stable. It's why big plans for change are so challenging for people either socially, domestically or at work. And when you think of large organisations, well . . . change can be extremely difficult to achieve.

Mini habits take very little willpower to do each day, to the point that you can do them even when you don't feel like it. And because they're so small, you can easily develop more than one at a time.

I had decided that I wanted to read before sleeping and go to bed earlier. Just one chapter a night was the mini habit I wanted to acquire. Sometimes, of course, I read more than that but the outcome of establishing that habit is that I now can't sleep without a book at my side. If I don't have one, I will download one or buy one at the airport. It would be unthinkable for me to be book-free.

I also wanted to be in bed before midnight. So instead of finalising what I was doing at 12, I started to get ready for bed at 11pm. A little more time for reading, more hours sleep, with additional advantages of sleeping more speedily and more deeply as a result of being more relaxed.

Four or five small habits can be targeted at the same time, but of course each person will be different so trial and error is useful. An example of a Mini Habit Regime might be:

- Drink a glass of water every morning.
- Stretch after getting out of bed.
- Floss every evening.
- Walk up the stairs instead of taking the lift.

But just like the parents of Marcus, consistency is vital. Don't miss days, even if you are on holiday, travelling, working late or returning home from a nearby swimming pool to one further afield!

Research confirms this proposition. Stewart Alexander and colleagues at Duke University Medical Center recorded the visits of 461 overweight or obese patients to their primary care physicians. The researchers recorded whether a physician had provided advice about weight loss or nutrition or physical activity, or a combination of all three. Patients who received all three types of advice during the same visit were the most likely to decrease their fat intake and lose weight. Surprisingly, patients who received only exercise advice were more likely to gain weight than patients who received no advice at all!

In another study, researchers examined the effect of an intervention to promote multiple health-related behaviours in couples aged 35 to 50 years. Participants were randomly assigned either to receive eight coun-selling sessions on physical activity, healthy diet, cancer screenings or alcohol use or to get advice on a combination of all four. A year later, those who had received combined lifestyle counselling were 40% more likely than those in the other groups to report increasing fruit and vegeta-ble consumption and physical activity. Cancer screening rates rose in the combined group, too.

The message from this recent research is that all of us can change mul-tiple health-related behaviours at once. And, in fact, tackling all at the same time actually works better perhaps because each change reinforces the others or you notice more progress more swiftly and that is hugely rewarding.

ALTERNATIVELY, START BIG

Success in overcoming one major limiting habit can also lead to the confidence to tackle many others in a short space of time. Psychologists would call it generalisation: one piece of behaviour changed leads to using the same methods to change the rest. In other words, you're on a roll.

I was asked by the BBC to take part in the programme "So You Think You're A Good Driver". A woman called Susan had contacted the programme asking for help to drive again after being off the road for eight years. She so feared having an accident that she had stopped driving or even being a passenger. The motivation for her Willpower Challenge was that her daughter had moved house and she had to take a train and two buses to see her and her grandchildren. The journey by car would be 30 minutes, but by public transport it was taking two and a half hours.

So here I was travelling by rail towards Birmingham with a television crew, knowing that I had to establish a fearless driving habit in place of an eight-year pattern of avoidance . . . and all in one day.

I learned that Susan's fear was around the sounds of crashing, especially the scrape of metal against metal, but when asked if she had ever experienced this she said she had not. I used the psychological principles of desensitisation: starting with easier activities then working up to the major concerns. For her, the list started with just looking at the family car on the road outside the house, then sitting in the driver's seat, driving to the corner of the road, then ultimately driving on a dual carriageway and motorway, then finally the journey to her daughter. A cluster of escalating habits.

Before embarking on this programme, I trained her in relaxation and visualisation. While in a relaxed state, she visualised all of the steps on her list and in this way achieved mastery mentally before the reality of driving.

When the time came to drive, all went well with the short distances but she did become a little wobbly coming up to traffic lights. She worried about stalling and creating mayhem behind her on the road. She mastered this by simply slowing the car down, relaxing at the lights and letting the cars behind take care of themselves. The outcome from all of this practice was that she drove so fast with a camera crew in pursuit that she lost them en route. She had quite forgotten she was part of a TV programme and was on the way to her daughter.

Although Susan's Willpower Challenge was big for her, all the steps to success were small – and she managed them all in a day.

The real purpose of telling you this story was because Susan had other avoidance habits. She refused invitations to parties as she hated balloons and their ability to burst in her face, and she also hid under the stairs with the dog during firework displays. Using the step-by-step process I taught her, as well as relaxation and visualisation, Susan then confronted her other issues. She called me a month later to say that as soon as she had mastered her biggest fear of driving, she knew she could destroy the others using exactly the same methods. Parties and firework displays are now on her social calendar.

So sometimes it's good to go big as nothing else can be so bad!

BECOMING FAILURE PROOF

The most predictable part of any Willpower Challenge is that you will fail, be tempted, will backslide at some point.

You will need a back-up plan just in case. We now know that habits are really sticky things – they don't disappear that easily, especially if they are well established. Avoiding some situations when you might be tempted, or surrounding yourself with like-minded people or distracting yourself, will all be strategies you can use.

Complete the checklist here to help you become failure proof with your Willpower Challenge:

Actions for Willpower: Failure Proof Checklist
- When might I be tempted to give in?
- What can I do to get away from temptation?
- What friend can I call for support?
- What do I actually say to myself when I pause and plan?
- If I have an extinction burst, what can I do to get back on track quickly?
- How can I forgive myself for a blip in my Willpower Challenge?

Forgiveness
No one is perfect, so expect to backslide occasionally during the first three weeks of behaviour change – and perhaps again in the ensuing nine weeks if you have an extinction burst. Have a plan in place, forgive yourself and move on.

Studies have looked at the effect of self-criticism, that internal "beating yourself up", on willpower. The long and the short of it is: it doesn't work. It gets you down and is associated with symptoms of depression. Willpower is never about perfection but about trying and learning.

Research was carried out this year, and reported by Psychblog (an online update of psychological research), into the hypothesis that working on self-esteem was the best way to move on from having regrets about failure.

One group was encouraged to boost their self-esteem with this direction:

> "Imagine you are talking to yourself about a regret from the perspective of boosting your positive qualities."

A second group was instructed:

> "Imagine you are talking to yourself about this regret from a compassionate and understanding perspective."

It was the second group who wrote self-compassionately that felt more self-forgiveness, personal improvement and acceptance. Self-compassion allows us to confront our regrets and view them rationally, so understanding our flaws is better than trying to boost our self-esteem via our positive qualities. This has its place, of course, but not while getting over failure.

Actions for Willpower
- Become self-aware about the habits you have learned from your parents.
- Understand habit formation and realise you are in charge of how you respond.
- It takes three weeks to change a behaviour and another nine weeks of repetition to turn that new behaviour into a habit.
- Extinction bursts need to recognised and defeated: get back on track quickly and don't give up, it's part of the Willpower process.
- Be consistent when establishing a habit.
- Replace a bad habit with a good new one.
- Become failure proof with a plan.
- Forgiveness works when mistakes happen: get back on track even stronger than before.

ELITE PERFORMERS AND 10 000 HOURS OF REPETITION

We have learned that new behaviour takes three weeks to establish and another nine weeks of repetition to create a habit; but if you want to be really successful at a habit, then you require 10 000 hours of repetition – according to Malcolm Gladwell in his book *Outliers – The Story of Success* (see Figure 3.5). He discusses the 1990s research by Anders Ericsson at the Berlin Academy of Music.

The study looked at three groups of violinists: those who were destined for world-class soloist careers, those who were good, and finally violinists who might teach rather than perform. All were asked how long they practised. They started playing at about the same age, around 5, but by 8 years old those who would go on to be star performers practised more and more until they were playing violin for more than 30 hours a week, which by the time they were 20 amounted to 10 000 hours. Amateurs played in comparison three hours a week, which totalled to 2000 hours.

Nicola Benedetti is 28, half-Scottish, half-Italian and was brought up in West Kilbride, Scotland. She followed her elder sister into playing the violin at just 4, and left Scotland to study at the Yehudi Menuhin School when she was 10. She won the BBC Young Musician of the Year award for her performance of Karol Szymanowski's *Violin Concerto No. 1*. She is very popular internationally, so keeping up with practising is difficult with her travel schedule and multiple engagements. She agrees that it is a challenge, but claims that this is not her main difficulty. She says that her inner hearing has an ideal and what she is constantly trying to do is work out how, physically, to get to that place. Most of the time she feels like she falls short of what her ear is looking for. She is a perfectionist.

Nicola has the looks of a pop star but she is committed to her craft and admits to practising up to six hours a day. I had the joy of hearing her play at a small dinner party and so I took the opportunity to talk to her after her performance. Musicianship is not habitual in her family: her father is an entrepreneur and neither parent plays an instrument. She did, however, learn the habit of hard work from both parents.

She emphasised that although her life looks glamorous, she has to practise every day to keep up to her own exacting standards. "The only time I'm really unhappy is when I pick up my violin and I think I really sound bad. My happiness does depend on that. If 24 hours go by and I haven't worked out how to get myself playing better again I'm just distraught, like life is going to end."

So, at age 28, playing six hours a day from let's say the age of 10, adds up to around 42 000 hours. You really do have to love what you do to practise your habit that much, but it makes you and keeps you first class.

Another example cited by Gladwell in his book is the story of the Beatles' rise to fame.

The Beatles

In 1960, The Beatles were a struggling rock back band in Liverpool when they were invited to play in Hamburg, Germany. They performed in a club which delivered a non-stop rock show. Because of this, the band was forced to play continuously for up to eight hours a night, seven days a week. They gained confidence, as they were reportedly rubbish initially, and they had to learn a huge repertoire of music, only latterly writing their own. Very few other bands have ever played so much for so long. When they achieved worldwide success in 1964 they had played 1200 times.

So we can deduce from this that repetition of a magnitude works. But, not so fast.

A new Princeton study reveals that hours of practice only accounted for a 12% difference in performance over various domains. Practice seems to work as a predictor of success when the rules are in a steady state as in, for example, chess, tennis, classical music, but perhaps not in the dotcom world of entrepreneurship.

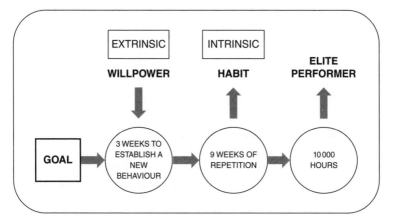

FIGURE 3.5 Habit and 10 000 hours

Are we saying here that no innate talent is necessary? That doing something, anything, for 10 000 hours is enough to become an expert?

This 10 000 hours rule goes back to Anders Ericsson in 1993 studying violin students; but he is now saying that the quality of practice is important, not just any old practice. So natural talent has to be there as a starting point. However, if like Nicola Benedetti you are still practising up to six hours per day, you must have to love what you do as well. Talent, love and practice for elite performance. Now there's a Willpower Challenge for you!

Good Habits for Bad

I thought if changing lifestyle habits was on your Willpower Challenge list, then I should discuss the universally known good ones with tips for replacing bad ones. We know the statistics, we read daily about new research with constant advertising on social media urging us towards a sleeker, happier, calmer version of ourselves. And some of that evidence is contradictory.

So I have drawn up a simple checklist (see Figure 3.6) with the major differentiators of a healthy existence. If you have any "no" responses, then add them to your Willpower Challenge list to be slotted into your programme at some point.

The Good Habits Checklist		
1	Do you sleep for seven or eight hours per night?	
	Yes	No
2a	Do you eat at least five portions of fruit and vegetables each day?	
	Yes	No
2b	Do you limit the amount of sugar and salt in your diet?	
	Yes	No
3	Are you able to reduce your alcohol intake when necessary?	
	Yes	No
4	Do you brush and floss your teeth every day?	
	Yes	No
5	Do you exercise at least three times per week?	
	Yes	No

FIGURE 3.6 Good Habits Checklist

GOOD HABITS MADE EASY

Sleep

Sleep is important to our functioning and to willpower. Sleep deprivation – getting less than six hours a night – impairs how the body and brain use energy. The prefrontal cortex is especially affected and loses control over the regions of the brain that create cravings and the stress response.

Insomniacs often develop strange habits at bedtime when they don't sleep. They surround themselves with books, magazines, music, TV and videos. These are all things to keep you awake rather than help you to fall asleep. Insomniacs will often go to bed earlier and earlier just in case sleep might catch them unawares.

Beds must be associated with relaxation, not stimulation, for a sleeping pattern to be established.

What stresses insomniacs is the fear of not functioning the following day, and that very thought keeps them awake. You can, of course, function without sleep on the odd occasion without too much suffering, as you can catch up on sleep the following night with little lasting effect, but with long-term insomnia, your decision making and daily functioning will be impaired. I have experienced this personally, and here are the tips that now ensure I can sleep anywhere on anything.

Tips

1. Place an alarm clock some distance away so that when not sleeping or wakening in the middle of the night, the time can't be seen. Unhelpful thoughts like "Oh no, it's 3am and there are only four hours to go before I get up" are counterproductive to relaxation and sleep. One night of restive sleep is really not a problem as you will make it up the next. It is a pattern of insomnia that is more challenging.
2. Turn off televisions, iPads, computers and mobile phones. The blue light they emit is not conducive to relaxation and winding down. Avoid catching up with Facebook, LinkedIn, Pinterest, Instagram or any other social media outlet that is the current thing as the

content, as well as the screen, energises. Read a book with real pages or a dimmed version of a Kindle or other reader.

3.   Limit the drinking of tea, coffee, chocolate, or Coca Cola after 2pm. They all act as stimulants with a half-life of six to eight hours. In other words, it takes that amount of time for the caffeine to leave your body. No more than two or three cups of substances containing caffeine should be imbibed during the day. Caffeine is helpful before a run or workout as there is evidence that it enables increased energy. Additional research has revealed that caffeine increases cognitive acuity – you think more clearly – and may mitigate the symptoms of Alzheimer's disease in later life. There are many positive effects, just don't imbibe it in the afternoon or evening.

4.   One to two hours before retiring to bed should be winding down time. The expectation that a high rate of activity can be immediately followed by sleep is a ridiculous thought. Working before going to bed, or indeed in bed, will stimulate your brain instead of slowing it down ready for sleep.

5.   If you are tossing and turning, do not continue this beyond 15–20 minutes. Get out of bed and sit in a chair and read, doze or use relaxation exercises. Bed must be associated with sleep and relaxation, not restlessness and insomnia.

6.   Even if you are having fitful sleep, resist napping during the day. This will disrupt your sleep pattern as the whole idea is to move towards a habitual sleep pattern. Try to get up at the same time every day despite the hours slept – even at weekends. This again allows a regular sleep pattern to become established.

7.   Use the Power Minute before sleeping (see the instructions that follow). This will induce not only a greater quantity, but also a better quality of sleep.

8.   If your mind is active with issues of the day, keep a notepad by your bed to jot ideas down. You will then relax and sleep with a clear mind. There is always something therapeutic about writing things down. Getting it out of your head and down on paper objectifies and clarifies.

9.   Take time to buy a bed, pillows and bedclothes that suit you. Try a bed out in the shop before buying. Not all beds and mattresses are the same, so invest in a good one. Turn a mattress over at least every two months as it will become lumpy and also requires airing. Change a mattress every eight years.

The Power Minute

Take the **One-Minute Breathing Test**. Time yourself for a minute and count your breaths – in and out is one.

Between 10 and 12 is an average number of breaths for normal breathing. More than that and you are breathing too rapidly and your breathing might be too shallow. It is not so much that you are not taking in enough oxygen, but more that you are not breathing out sufficient carbon dioxide.

When tense, your breathing tends to speed up automatically. By slowing it down you also decrease your heart and pulse rate. Breathing out is the crucial part of the process as it rids the lungs of stale air, stops you feeling dizzy and, as a result, muscles are less cramped and sore.

Repeat the **One-Minute Breathing Test** again, this time breathing in and out more slowly while allowing yourself to let go and slow down. This more relaxed breathing constitutes the **Power Minute** and it will energise you. It is only a minute so even the most stressed can make time. If you are working late then the Power Minute will help to identify priorities and increase concentration so that you can spend less time at your desk. Use the Power Minute on a regular basis.

More relaxation techniques are available to download free from www .rostaylorcompany.com/relaxation. You will be sent a link to save on mobile or tablet. It takes three weeks to learn these new relaxation skills when you practise every day and another nine weeks to turn this new behaviour into a habit.

Follow this advice and you will look forward to bedtime and a good eight hours' sleep. You will feel comforted and cosseted at night: rested and energised in the morning.

Food

More fruit and vegetables, more fibre, less salt and sugar, cut down on fats and carbs (see Figure 3.7). Not rocket science. We all know this advice yet we still don't follow it. Habits learned at home die hard.

When I started working in television I decided to go on a diet. The screen does add an extra dress size after all! But there were always the best sandwiches in the Green Room where guests and staff congregated before the nightly news programme. It was, I told myself, extra fuel before the rigours of live performance. An essential. But these sandwiches were jeopardising my diet. So my Willpower Challenge was to

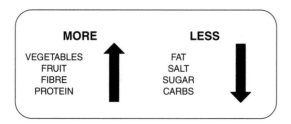

FIGURE 3.7 A Simple Good Food Guide

replace the carbohydrates with a large glass of water and some fruit. After 12 weeks I didn't notice them and never really enjoyed sandwiches again.

Tips

1. Read labels in supermarkets. Look for low fat, low sugar, low salt alternatives.
2. Eat before shopping. If you're hungry this will influence your choices and you are more likely to regress towards high-calorie comfort food and old habits.
3. Buy fresh food to cook yourself, as then you know the contents of the dish. Instant meals contain a plethora of ingredients designed to be tasty but are destined to undermine your diet.
4. Don't buy biscuits and chocolates. If they are around you WILL eat them. Not today perhaps, but at some time in the near future.
5. Don't make the excuse that the kids like sugary, salty, fatty stuff so you have to buy it. You are the parent and you are helping them develop habits they will find difficult to undo in later life.
6. Eat less and you will lose weight.

Comedienne Viv Groskop talks about how she lost three stone in a year. She has a number of rules for weight loss and exercise: no white carbs, no processed food, measure yourself every two weeks (scales and tape measure), exercise hard three times a week, less or no alcohol and "don't tell people as they will try to make you have fun instead!". It should be made easy, she says. Keep your exercise clothes beside your bed. Roll over and get into them or even wear them to sleep! Hand over your exercise regime to a professional and keep repeating it, as it's all about habit. She concludes: "Don't always expect to enjoy it. Do it to be healthy and not die so soon!"

Alcohol

We read about Grace and her Willpower Challenge earlier in the book. She gave up alcohol so that her son would not be brought up by an alcoholic mother. The vast majority of people are not abusing alcohol to that extent, but they may want to cut back for the sake of their livers.

It can be a bit tricky to understand and remember how much alcohol is in drinks, and how this can affect our health. The low-risk guidelines can help with this.

No one can say that drinking alcohol is absolutely safe, but by sticking within these guidelines, you can lower your risk of harming your health if you drink most weeks:

Tips

1. Know your units. Men and women are advised not to drink more than 14 units a week. Spread your drinking over three days or more if you drink as much as 14 units a week (see Figure 3.8).
2. If you want to cut down how much you're drinking, a good way to help achieve this is to have several drink-free days each week.
3. Once you've got the hang of the low-risk guidelines, then check how many units are in your usual tipple. "ABV" means the percentage of alcohol in the drink and you can often find this information on the side of the bottle or can. The amount of alcohol in drinks can vary quite widely, and it's worth looking for versions of your favourite drinks that have less alcohol, which can also be cheaper and often contain fewer calories.
4. Drink more slowly, putting your glass down in between sips.
5. Drink water in between glasses of spirits or wine.
6. Add ice cubes to alcohol, even wine. It dilutes the strength and the drink lasts longer . . . and keeps cool.
7. If suffering any hangover effects, cut back.

> **Medical Warning**
>
> If you have physical withdrawal symptoms (like shaking, sweating, or feeling anxious until you have your first drink of the day) you should take medical advice before stopping completely as it can be dangerous to do this too quickly without proper advice and support.

HOW MUCH IS 14 UNITS IN REAL DRINKS?

The following is a general guide – actual levels will vary depending on
the strength of the drink and the size of the serving:

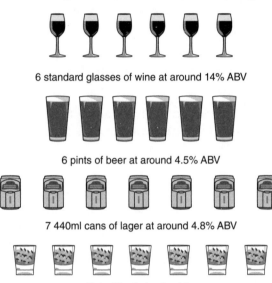

6 standard glasses of wine at around 14% ABV

6 pints of beer at around 4.5% ABV

7 440ml cans of lager at around 4.8% ABV

7 double shots of spirits

Figures from Alcohol Research UK, January 2016

FIGURE 3.8 A Simple Guide to Units of Alcohol

Teeth

The state of your teeth affects your overall health, with gum disease
linked to lots of health problems in other parts of the body. For example, it may increase the risk of stroke, diabetes, heart disease and is
even associated with problems in pregnancy and dementia. Therefore, brushing your teeth regularly has quite astonishing multiple
benefits.

Chief Executive of the British Dental Health Foundation, Dr Nigel Carter,
explains: "The link between oral health and overall body health is well
documented and backed by robust scientific evidence. Despite this,
only one in six people realise that people with gum disease may have an
increased risk of stroke or diabetes. And only one in three is aware of the
heart disease link."

In the US recently, when counting the cost of all the cumulative research over the years into diabetes, stroke and heart disease, they concluded that the best preventative aid, more effective and very much cheaper than all others, was to send a toothbrush to all households and encourage regular use.

Tips
1. Go to the dentist regularly, every six months.
2. Buy an electric toothbrush.
3. Brush three times a day. Brush your teeth especially in the morning to rid your mouth of toxins built up overnight.
4. Floss regularly.

Exercise
Does going to the gym bore you? Does running fill you with dread? Is the sweatiness of the whole thing a complete turn off?

Well, some new work with Mindfulness suggests that there are two strategies to help you.

1. What is it that you hate? What makes you uncomfortable? Once you are aware of what is off-putting, then you can come to terms with the associated physical sensations.
2. Focus on the outcomes of exercise and the plentiful benefits which provide meaning to exercising.

And there are myriad positive outcomes revealed in the *British Journal of Health Psychology* concerning a study of students who went from no exercise to a modest programme of gym visits two or three times per week. They experienced:

- A decrease in stress, smoking, alcohol and caffeine consumption.
- An increase in healthy eating, better spending and working habits and feeling more comfortable at uncomfortable times.

Charles Duhigg in his book *The Power of Habit* calls exercise a keystone habit; in other words, a change in one part of your life leads to positive changes in another. He says, "exercise changes our sense of self and our sense of what is possible".

Tips
1. Start small with one push up, one length of the swimming pool, a short walk at lunch time.

2. Choose some form of exercise you might actually like or dislike less than others. Dancing, Zumba, weightlifting, walking, anything that increases your heart rate.
3. Exercise with other like-minded people. Everything is easier with support.
4. Focus on why you are doing it. Have the reward firmly in your mind as an end-point.

All of the above lifestyle changes also have an impact on Willpower. The healthier you are, the better rested you feel, the more prepared you are for anything your Willpower Challenge can throw at you.

This is a good point to bring in *Phil Howard*, award-winning chef of the top London restaurant The Square and a former drug addict.

> *"Ultimately, willpower comes in trying to stop yourself doing something that you're otherwise wanting to do, where the temptation lies. The reality is that addiction is cunning, it's baffling, drugs are immensely compulsive and while willpower alone is absolutely not the solution to long-term abstinence, it absolutely does play a part in the early days of keeping you out of trouble. This sheer ability to withstand a craving for whatever is your drug of choice is critical in those early days, coming to realise all cravings, all feelings, all emotions pass with time. The ability to sit out the compulsion to use drugs is critical in the early days while you build the other side of the equation, which is the immediate benefit of not doing so and the sense of self-worth that comes with that. When using drugs, there's a huge amount of damage to your self-worth and until that's built up again, willpower plays a huge part in restoring your sense of pride in being.*
>
> *One of the things I've learned in life is that it's ok to be wrong. I just make decisions, and I make lots of good ones and I also get things wrong but I'm not the sort of person who beats myself up; as long as I'm generally heading in the right direction and learn from my mistakes I'm un-phased. Acceptance is the key to everything, whatever it might be, and is the key to change. You've got to be able to love yourself a bit to be able to move on.*
>
> *Now I exercise. Even when it's pelting with rain, I don't allow myself to turn back. On the whole, I have come to learn that the benefits of running are massive, even when it's just routine jogging, running*

along the river because I want to keep in good shape and there's no particular training going on. I just know that if I go out for a run, I'll be a better and happier human being. It's very rare that I'll back out of a run.

Going outside, going for a quick walk, these are habits that I learned in the early days of recovery and quitting drugs. If I shut the curtains, eat a packet of chocolate biscuits and watch some crap on TV, it's a negative scenario, but if I get out and do some good, giving time to other people for example, then in the end that becomes a habit."

"Between stimulus and response there is a space . . . In that space is our power to choose our response. In our response lies our growth and our freedom."

—*Viktor Frankl*

Man's Search for Meaning

REMINDERS

- Replace bad habits with good ones.
- Use willpower for three weeks to establish the new routine or behaviour.
- Repeat for another nine weeks, give or take, to produce a new habit.
- Repeat for another 10 000 hours to become an elite musician, athlete or professional something.
- You can choose a variety of small habits to change or indeed one huge one that will make a huge difference.
- Core habits to lengthen your life are sleeping for seven or eight hours, healthy eating, moderate alcohol consumption, exercising three times a week as well as brushing and flossing your teeth.
- Look out for extinction bursts and don't capitulate.
- Forgive yourself for mistakes and get back on track.

Congratulations for getting so far in the book. You are exchanging good habits for bad, old with new for three weeks and another nine. Turn to Part Four to secure a willpower mindset which will help maintain your willpower for ever.

PART FOUR

The Willpower Mindset

I asked Judy Murray, mother of tennis champions Andy and Jamie Murray, what it was that made her sons so successful and what made her such a supportive parent.

She had always loved the sport, she said, and when the boys were young they were given tennis rackets and played with her and each other. Jamie is the eldest, so for Andy it was hugely important that he become as good as his older brother. They were always very competitive with each other.

Five out of six children who played at an under-10s competition with Andy and Jamie have now taken part in Wimbledon (for example, Jamie Baker and Natasha Khan); however, it was Andy who showed the most singles promise. He complained to his mother that he wanted to compete rather than just playing tennis continuously with her and his brother. Subsequently, he played in a competition with Rafael Nadal in his teens and heard about Nadal's attendance at a Spanish tennis coaching school and, of course, nothing would do until he went too. Somehow the Murrays scraped together the money and he was there for over two years. He and Rafa have been friends for life as a result.

When he was 18 Andy was in the ATP finals, so suddenly he was on the radar as an upcoming player. And in 2007 Jamie won the mixed doubles at Wimbledon with a partner he just met when he arrived. The rest is history.

And of course Judy is a force in tennis and the media in her own right now. We have seen her performance in "Strictly Come Dancing". She said: "Great fun for someone who could never dance." She is also a tennis coach for Scotland. She and a colleague drive around in a van training teachers and sport coaches how to coach tennis. To date she has trained 3500 people and returns every three to four months to top up their skills.

She was the women's coach for the Aegon tennis team in 2011 and revealed that there are very few resources in the UK for women's tennis. Investment is in the men's game and focused on England. Scotland gets a fraction of the money but has produced the majority of the talent. So her persistence and willpower in the face of financial strictures have been nothing short of amazing. "When you have no money you find a way of doing what you can with very little."

So I then asked her what created the huge success her sons have had. She said that they both just love the sport, love the challenge and love the competitive nature of it. Both her sons come from a background of challenge where money was in short supply, so nothing was taken for granted and everything came with effort. She said that both Andy and Jamie have *mental toughness* and *tremendous willpower* to cope with the challenge of it all. When Andy lost Wimbledon he hibernated for four days because he was so upset and felt he had let everyone down. That phase had to be short-lived as he was scheduled to start preparing for the Olympics immediately. Emerge he did, and went on to win a gold medal for Britain. Subsequently he won the US Open with two Wimbledon titles and Davies Cup wins to follow – and as of November 2016 he's the number 1 tennis player in the world!

For Judy – well she just loves a challenge. She said: "If I'm told I can't do something I just go out and prove them wrong." The boys have certainly learned willpower from their mother.

SO HOW CAN WE ALL ACQUIRE A MURRAY MINDSET?

This chapter will outline the ingredients of a willpower mindset and help you personalise any changes you might have to make. At the end of Part One, I introduced the research results of Veronika Job, Carol Dweck and Gregory Walton, which show that your belief about willpower determines whether willpower becomes depleted. So having a willpower mindset that overcomes hurdles means that you don't need to be fed sugar lumps, energy drinks or limit yourself to completing one challenge at a time in case you become exhausted. This frees up lots of possibilities.

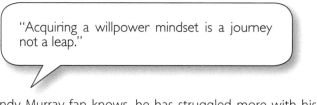

"Acquiring a willpower mindset is a journey not a leap."

As any Andy Murray fan knows, he has struggled more with his thinking rather than his physical ability. It has certainly been a journey for him which he seems to be winning. The evidence for the onlooker is seeing him between sets looking at pre-prepared notes reminding him how to achieve positive focus. Thoughts are powerful.

Achieving a "can do" mindset, though of course doable, may need some work to change an already established pattern. Yes – it's another habit to replace. Our thoughts are not that easy to change, especially if we have thought them for a long time. So three weeks for a new thinking style and another nine for habit forming is again the routine.

Thinking

Aaron Beck is a famous cognitive therapist, but back in the days when he was using psychoanalytic techniques he discovered, during free association (sessions where patients are asked to talk about anything that comes into their heads), the existence of another type of thinking he called *automatic thinking.*

Here he tells of his discovery. This extract is from *Cognitive Therapy and the Emotional Disorders.*

> *"These automatic thoughts reported by numerous patients had a number of characteristics in common. They generally were not vague and unformulated, but were specific and discrete. They occurred in a kind of shorthand; that is only the essential words in a sentence seemed to occur – as in a telegraphic style. Moreover, these thoughts did not arise as a result of deliberation, reasoning or reflection about an event or topic. There was no logical sequence of steps such as in goal-orientated thinking or problem solving. The thoughts 'just happened' as if by reflex. They seemed to be relatively autonomous, in that the patient made no effort to initiate them and, especially in the more disturbed cases, they were difficult to 'turn off'. In view of their involuntary quality they could just as well have been labelled 'autonomous thoughts' as automatic thoughts.*
>
> *In addition, the patient tended to regard these automatic thoughts as plausible or reasonable, although they may have seemed far-fetched*

to somebody else. The patients accepted their validity without ques-
tion and without testing out their reality or logic. Of course, many of
these thoughts were realistic, but the patient often tended to believe
the unrealistic thoughts, even though they had decided during previ-
ous discussions that they were invalid. When he took time out to
reflect on their validity or discussed their validity with me, he would
conclude they were invalid. Yet, the next time that he had the same
automatic thought, he would tend to accept it at face value."

The automatic thoughts which Beck describes comprise the inner dialogue which continues in our heads even as we are talking about something completely different. This dialogue can propel us to great things or talk us out of new situations and challenges. The latter thinking is not easy to change, but changed it can be. And as soon as you embark on this transformation you will feel and act in a much more energetic and purposeful way.

So let's get started by identifying any unhelpful thinking (see Figure 4.1).

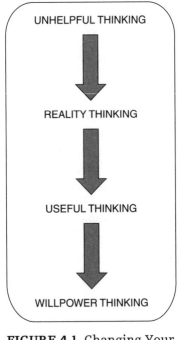

FIGURE 4.1 Changing Your
Thinking

Negative Thinking

Labelling Let's begin to tap into *your* thoughts and thinking styles. Be as honest as possible and complete the following exercise. I would like you to make a list of five words, phrases or traits that describe you best:

1. As you see yourself.
2. The view of a superior or stakeholder at work.
3. The view of a relative or partner.

The Labelling Exercise

Use five words, phrases or traits to describe you:

1. As you see yourself:

   I am _____

   I am _____

   I am _____

   I am _____

   I am _____

2. The view of a superior at work:

   I am _____

   I am _____

   I am _____

   I am _____

   I am _____

3. The view of a relative or partner:

   I am _____

   I am _____

   I am _____

   I am _____

   I am _____

When completed, judge whether your words, phrases or traits are positive or negative for each of the sections and place a plus or minus sign where relevant.

Reflect on the Following Questions:
1. Did you have more positives than negatives overall?
2. Did more negatives cluster in one section than others?
3. If you do have some negatives, why did you not consider a list of 15 positives? And if you did consider it, what stopped you writing them down?

This exercise strikes at the heart of self-esteem. If you have written 15 positive statements, well done. For those of you with some negatives, I am sure if I met you I could come up with 15 or more positive traits to describe you. So what stops your own positive self-appraisal? Humility? Upbringing? Culture? Perhaps a cocktail of all three.

Of course you have weaknesses, but all too often I'll bet you emphasise those at the expense of your strengths. And sometimes those perceived weaknesses have outgrown their usefulness and you have advanced in skills and confidence beyond that label. It's as if inside you, what you believe about yourself is slow to catch up with external reality. You have had these thoughts for so long they automatically, habitually come to mind when you think about yourself – the kind of thoughts Aaron Beck talked about.

Do you have any worn out, way past their sell-by-date labels? Check with friends and relatives, is this how they see you? Then, if these labels no longer hold water, throw them out. On the other hand, feedback from your nearest and dearest may reinforce some of your weaknesses and add a few more. If so, write the opposite beside the negative statement and make that a goal for change – if you want to change, of course. I say that advisedly as there may be some negative aspects you don't want to change, like working too hard or loving the detail of things.

David Schwartz in his book *The Magic of Thinking Big* talks about how we use labels as excuses for inaction. We are too tall, too short, too fat, too thin, too lively, too quiet, too anything to be successful. His advice is to get rid of the labels, get rid of the excuses. You can see the relevance for willpower. If your inner dialogue is around failure and fear of failure, then you might talk yourself out of your Willpower Challenge before you've even begun, and we can't have that.

Labels that are wrong or out of date are one example of unhelpful thinking. There are others.

Catastrophy Thinking Another type of unhelpful thinking is *catastrophy thinking*. In times of stress and change at home and at work these thoughts proliferate. Coffee rooms in businesses and offices must teem with exaggerated predictions of personal disaster as soon as the word "reorganisation" is mentioned. The fact that nothing, no matter how bad things get, comes near to these prognostications doesn't stop us indulging in such thoughts again and again. So why do we do it? Do we really believe it is the end of the world as we know it? The trick in overcoming this kind of thinking starts with catching yourself using words like awful, dreadful, disastrous and then asking yourself: how awful is this really? On a scale of 1 to 10, how bad is this? Your situation is unlikely to reach a 10 unless you are being held up by an armed assassin with a balaclava and sawn-off shotgun. Problem solved. Once you have relaxed a little, finding solutions and being creative become so much easier.

This thinking style was one of my favourites and I learned to do nothing, say nothing for 5 to 10 seconds until I had thought the issue through. If I have lost my purse, instead of looking at the people sitting next to me in the theatre as if they were thieves, I have learned to imagine calmly where I last saw it – probably in one of my many handbags!

> "Anxiety interrupts memory. Relaxation restores it."

Black and White Thinking Black and white thinking is the kind that goes hand in hand with perfectionism. It involves seeing the world as right or wrong with no shades of grey in between, as well as a "nothing's worth doing unless you do it well" philosophy. This all sounds terribly laudable until you see how limiting and stressful it is. In terms of willpower, it can lead to dropping out of a challenge at the first hurdle with thoughts of "I'm completely useless at this". Life is full of grey areas and mistakes are unimportant. You recover and move on. In fact, I think mistakes are rather endearing. This of course may be some idiosyncratic thinking on my part as I am constantly getting things wrong and completely forgetting things. I have often been known to ask an audience where I am during a speech as I've gone off on a tangent of a story. Usually someone's been listening . . . well, at least I work on that principle.

Over Generalising Over generalising is where, given one failure, you imagine you will only have others. At one end of the spectrum, over generalising can lead to phobias, like a fear of flying, when one bumpy flight leads to fears of the same happening again, so flying is avoided. I used to run a Fear of Flying course with British Airways some years ago and I remember Robert, a travel agent, who despite an array of free flight incentives just would not fly because he recalled a difficult landing 15 years previously and was convinced it would happen again. Changing his thinking to allow the possibility that his next flight might just be OK (or, if not, he would cope with it) was the turning point for him. Robert then proceeded to fly around the world sending postcards to my increasingly jealous team.

At the more everyday end of the spectrum, this thinking style may not be as dramatic as producing phobias but can be just as limiting. Putting yourself forward for promotion and being refused even an interview, auditioning for a principal role in the opera society to end up in the chorus or writing a novel and being rejected by the publisher; we have all been there. It is humiliating, embarrassing, upsetting. But if you ever find yourself saying "I'll never try that again", stop to ask if this is due to a reaction to failure or a genuine dislike of the activity. Failure is OK. It may not be pleasant and may even feel profoundly uncomfortable but it does not make you a bad person or a lesser being – just human.

Be upset. Don't cover up your disappointment or control your emotions. You get ulcers that way. And don't even do as I have done in the past and pretend you didn't want the job/part/publisher in the first place. That is simply dishonest and stops you learning.

Ask yourself: "Next time, how would I do things differently?" Or ask for advice. The people on the interview/auditioning/publishing panel could be extremely helpful in directing you to where you might improve your skills. If it helps, see yourself as a product requiring promotion or marketing, anything which stops you feeling destroyed as a person and increases your objectivity. As you overcome setbacks and your thinking becomes more robust, the less emotional you are and the faster your recovery from disappointment is.

Ignoring Positives When in the grip of *negative thinking* we tend to *ignore the positives*. Those of you with teenage children will know just what I mean. By the time they have not kept their room tidy for months, have strewn their dirty clothes around the house, repeatedly come in late, played loud music you hate and conversed in mono-syllables for at least a year, it is difficult to remember the loveable creatures they used to be. But of course they are rarely all bad. Look for the good and reward it.

One company director I was training in motivational skills said that he could cope with anyone and anything, but not his son George. George had all of the above bad habits and the audacity to want to be a musician rather than an accountant like his father. I asked him when he had last said anything positive to his son, and he was horrified to note it had been years. In fact, his son had made some attempts to foster a relationship with his father by inviting him to a concert and had recently offered to cook supper. All these overtures had been treated with disdain by a father who had fallen into a nega-tive mindset about anything his son did.

It is so easy to get into bad habits. At work especially, because you see the same people every day, it is particularly difficult to notice if anyone's behaviour has improved. Your initial negative perception of them tends to remain the same despite contrary evidence. The other awful thing that happens when a manager does change for the bet-ter after years of complaints from employees is that nobody notices or, even worse, they undermine the change.

Negatively Predicting the Future Another manifestation of faulty thinking is *negatively predicting the future*. This is especially a charac-teristic of people who call themselves worriers. They often have the notion of "once a worrier always a worrier", which is only true if you do nothing about it. All of us when we are in "worry mode" embark on a series of short negative thoughts that chain together – one lead-ing to another until we reach a final depressing scenario.

> "Thoughts are not facts – with practice you can change them."

And with that thought in mind, let's move on from the details of negative thinking to understanding the nature of optimism and pessimism and whether you are an optimist or a pessimist.

Pessimism

Martin Seligman supplied evidence of a long-term study he had undertaken in which he benchmarked a large group of people as optimists or pessimists based on the language they used during telephone calls, in letters and memos and their coffee room chat. He then followed them up over 20 years. These results were compelling. There were more positive thinkers alive at the end of the project than pessimists. Optimists were also more likely to be successful in all that they undertook, were less likely to have nasty life events and less likely to become depressed.

I realised that I needed to change. Optimism was not for "other people", this was for me, and what I required to move forward was the hard evidence that it worked. You get very used to the thinking style you employ because it is inside your head with no external repudiation. I was definitely a half empty person, who used little phrases like "with my luck I will fail" when sitting exams or "with my luck I will forget my words" when I was singing. I saw myself as accident prone rather than someone who coped with any adversity.

My humour was also embedded in negativity and messing up. It was about me being silly and accident prone, and I could recount numerous examples of saying the wrong thing or falling over at important moments. I began to realise that these stories were all about putting myself down before others could. When relinquishing negativity, this was the most difficult part to change.

The Seligman quote here gave me the expectation that I didn't have to be a negative thinker forever.

> "Habits of thinking need not be forever. One of the most significant findings in psychology in the last twenty years is that individuals can choose the way they think."
>
> —*Martin Seligman from* Learned Optimism

Complete *The Origins of Optimism* questionnaire given here to discover your thinking style. It is an adaptation of a much longer Seligman questionnaire. Circle options A or B for the 12 statements then score your results in Table 4.1. A positive score is achieved when your score matches the optimist choice.

The Origins of Optimism Questionnaire

1. You forgot a friend's birthday
   A. I'm not good at remembering birthdays
   B. I was preoccupied with other things
2. You run for a community post and get it
   A. I devote a lot of time and energy to campaigning
   B. I work hard at everything I do
3. You get lost driving to a friend's house
   A. I missed a turn
   B. My friend gave me bad directions
4. You are frequently asked to dance at a party
   A. I am outgoing at parties
   B. I was in perfect form that night
5. You miss an important engagement
   A. Sometimes my memory fails me
   B. I sometimes forget to check my diary
6. The project you are in charge of is a great success
   A. I kept a close watch over everyone's work
   B. Everyone devoted a lot of time and energy to it
7. You gain weight over the holidays and you can't lose it
   A. Diets don't work in the long run
   B. The diet I tried didn't work
8. A friend thanks you for getting him through a bad time
   A. I enjoy helping him through tough times
   B. I care about people
9. You buy your partner a present and they don't like it
   A. I don't put enough thought into things like that
   B. They have very picky tastes
10. You are asked to head up an important project
    A. I have just successfully completed another similar project
    B. I am a good supervisor
11. You lose at a sporting event for which you have been training for a long time
    A. I'm not very athletic
    B. I'm not good at that sport
12. You tell a joke and everyone laughs
    A. My timing was perfect
    B. The joke was funny

TABLE 4.1 Origins of Optimism Questionnaire Scoring

Scoring	Optimist choice	Your choice
1. Sometimes thinking for bad events	B	
2. Everywhere thinking for good events	B	
3. Not me thinking for bad events	B	
4. Always thinking for good events	A	
5. Specific thinking for bad events	B	
6. Me thinking for good events	A	
7. Sometimes thinking for bad events	B	
8. Everywhere thinking for good events	B	
9. Not me thinking for bad events	B	
10. Always thinking for good events	B	
11. Specific thinking for bad events	B	
12. Me thinking for good events	A	
Total of Matching Scores:		

Results

1. Scores between *10* and *12*. Congratulations! You are an optimist about events around you, good and bad, and an optimist about yourself.

2. Scores between *6* and *9*. You may have specific areas of pessimism in your thinking. Review your answers to find out if your pessimist answers are for always, everywhere or me thinking, or for good or bad circumstances. Reward yourself for your optimist answers.

3. Scores between *1* and *5*. You are more of a pessimist than an optimist. Review your answers to find out if your pessimist answers are for always, everywhere or me thinking, or for good or bad circumstances. Really consider if you beat yourself up when bad things happen and also rarely congratulate yourself when things go well. You may be a perfectionist, which in the past you may have found helpful; however, if it is undermining a positive view of yourself, then change your thinking.

Seligman's theory of learned optimism revolves around three thinking styles which I have converted to *always*, *everywhere* and *me thinking*. When good things happen to an optimist, they think that they are on a roll and this will not be contained to one area of their lives. It will generalise to everything they do and is very much due to them.

Three Thinking Styles

Always
Everywhere
Me

The opposite is experienced by the pessimist. They think that only sometimes for very specific circumstances will they succeed, and it is usually down to other people's involvement. Any success is attributed to a fluke, which may never happen again.

Looking at Table 4.1, you can see another reversal for bad events. The pessimist thinks that when bad things happen they are on the slippery slope to disaster with every aspect of their life affected – and it is all their fault. Contrarily, the optimist thinks that a bad event is a mere glitch and they will be fine in a moment, telling themselves that loads of people were involved in that screw up not just them.

Thinking for Good Events
   The **pessimist** thinks:
 • they *sometimes*
 • in *specific* circumstances might succeed
 • and *"it's probably a fluke."*
   The **optimist** thinks:
 • they *always*
 • in *every* part of their life will succeed
 • and *"it's all due to me."*

Thinking for Bad Events
   The **pessimist** thinks:
 • they *always*
 • in *every* part of their life will fail in some way
 • and *"it's all my fault."*
   The **optimist** thinks:
 • they *sometimes*
 • in *some* circumstances might fare less well
 • and *"it may be nothing to do with me."*

Review your scores and reward yourself for the areas in which you are optimistic and list those which require work. People are often surprised by this questionnaire, as they have viewed themselves as positive thinkers but may achieve a low score here. The major area is the "me" section. You may be optimistic about events but shy away from patting yourself on the back for successes or beat yourself up when things go wrong.

Participants on my Leadership Programme who complete this questionnaire often complain that it would be arrogant to say that you have played a major part in successes. Surely it is about celebrating a team effort, all for one and one for all, they say. Of course, it would be good leadership to reward the team, but you can still tell *yourself* that you were the main coordinator/contributor. In the still of the night you can smile and feel good. There is no crime in that.

Having discovered that I was optimistic about my clients and colleagues but not about myself, my life or my work, I realised I had much to change. First to go was what I said to myself all the time, my inner dialogue. Out went "with my luck I will mess up" and in came phrases which work for me, for example "I am OK, I will cope" not "I'm fabulous" or "I'm the best", but "I'm OK". Anything more seemed overinflated to my Scottish psyche.

Every morning I would sit at the end of my bed visualising the day ahead. For example: it is 10am and my first meeting is finished and it has gone well; it is now midday and my presentation to the board of the bank has been successful and they want additional coaching for 20 staff; lunch with the partners and they are discussing the successful allocation of the project to my company . . . and so on. As a result of this hard work, sitting on the edge of the bed every morning for three weeks with another nine of repeating this thinking every day, I now rarely imagine anything going wrong in my life or work. And if it does, I know I will cope.

In this part of the book, I have discussed unhelpful thinking and how you change that and have outlined Seligman's work on optimistic and pessimistic thinking. If you have positive inner dialogue and achieved a score of 12 on the Optimism Scale, then good for you. This will be so helpful for your Willpower Challenge. You will go forward with purpose and positivity. There may be others of you who identified some habitual unhelpful thoughts and a tendency towards pessimism. Help is here.

Actions for a Willpower Mindset
- Identify any negative thinking you might have: negative labelling, catastrophy or black and white thinking, over generalising, ignoring positives or negatively predicting the future.
- Remember: thoughts are not facts. You can change them.

- Discover whether you are an optimist or a pessimist.
- When things are going badly, realise there may be many reasons for this. When things are going well, you have been instrumental in that success.
- You have the power to change your inner dialogue to be positive.

REALITY THINKING

What characterises all faulty thinking and pessimism is its emotionality and lack of objectivity. It is also very egocentric; a whirlpool of negativity, and is entirely self-focused. Questioning this thinking, looking for evidence that might support or refute your perceptions, helps to objectify and realistically evaluate these thoughts.

Follow the directions below with a less than successful event in mind.

Evidence
a.   What evidence is there to support your thoughts about the event?
b.   What evidence is there to contradict them?

You need to become a researcher and experimenter with your own mindset. Be evidential. Remember, your thoughts are not facts, so create some objectivity about your thinking.

A young woman was referred to me as she had a problem with blushing. It was limiting her work prospects as she avoided meetings, especially presentations. I suggested relaxation techniques, strategies to cope when she could feel a blush coming on, and paradoxical intention where I got her to try to blush on demand, which of course she couldn't. But the major game changer was when she asked colleagues if they had noticed her blushing. They had not. They thought she looked pleasantly flushed. She had spent years worrying while all along no one had noticed.

- Ask those around you for confirmation of your doubts and thoughts. Are they indeed correct or is your perception skewed?
- Write things down and ask yourself if you can solve these issues or if you have to cope emotionally and get on with your life.
- Anything which externalises your thinking, exposes it to the cold light of day, is helpful here. The externalisation process of reality thinking is the essence of rationality and objectivity which can keep you on track. Of course, if it is your fault, then you can decide to problem solve or emotionally cope.

Alternatives
  a.   How would you advise someone else in this situation?
  b.   How might someone else react in this situation?
  c.   What evidence is there now to support alternatives?

We are so speedy to supply advice to others. I know this to be true, especially when I run Corporate Coach International – my coaching school – training executives to become coaches. The poor client has hardly drawn a breath at the end of their story and my fledgling coaches are saying "what you need to do is . . .". It's a human trait to want to help and offer advice. So use this advice giving tendency for yourself. How might you advise someone else or how might someone you know react to the situation you face? That change of perspective helps.

Outcomes
  a.   What is your goal in the problem situation?
  b.   Does the negative interpretation help or hinder achieving the goal?
  c.   What might be the effect of believing an alternative?

Returning to your goals also recalibrates what you are thinking and doing. A favourite phrase of mine is "how helpful is my thinking right now to move me forward?" If the answer is "not very", stop it and find an alternative more helpful thought. I will bet the shift you feel will be a game changer. For willpower, returning all the time to remind yourself why you are undertaking a challenge is very important to your success.

I was speaking at a Leadership Conference and, prior to my speech, *Charlie Flynn* a young lightweight boxer aged 23 took to the stage and talked about his preparation for the Commonwealth Games in 2014.

For four years from age 16 Charlie ran every day from 6.30 to 9.30am and adhered to a strict diet to ensure his lightweight status. To accommodate this training schedule, he had to work part time in a Post Office sorting department earning £200 per week. This resulted in him taking out loans to survive. To rub salt into the wound, while his friends were out drinking with their girlfriends he was home alone, as he doesn't drink alcohol and training was taking up all his time.

He began to question where all this training was getting him, as well as the limitations imposed on his lifestyle, and he decided to give it all up. His parents, crucial motivators in his life, reminded him of his goal to win a medal and, as a result, his transgression lasted a matter of days and he was back on track, running through the streets of Lanark at 6.30am.

He stuck to his four-year plan and in 2014, aged 21, Charlie Flynn won the gold medal in the Lightweight Boxing Championships at the Commonwealth Games. He said, "people only see you winning, not the years of hard work and hardship. When you are on that podium receiving a gold medal all the hard work is worth it."

Learning
    a.   What have you learned?
    b.   What might you do differently next time?

Learning, constant learning. Willpower is part of a learning journey with a constant review of what works, what needs to be left behind and what has to be learned to move forward.

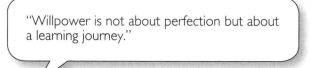

"Willpower is not about perfection but about a learning journey."

EXTERNALISE YOUR THINKING

Externalising your thinking is so important for your Willpower Challenge that I would like you to make a list of friends, colleagues and professional advisors who will have your best interests at heart *and* provide honest feedback, in the same way that Charlie Flynn had his parents at hand to help him get back with the programme. These people can include family, but be aware they might be very partisan and not, therefore, entirely balanced in their views. Use professionals for your list – lawyers, accountants, coaches or colleagues and a variety of friends.

You don't have to agree with all suggestions supplied by your supporters, but it is interesting to hear their point of view. The very process of asking objectifies your thinking and keeps you "cool".

Other Externalising Tricks:
- Write things down which are troubling you in the middle of the night. Then go to sleep after you have formulated your thoughts. When you look at the list in the morning, then everything seems more doable.
- Use this question: do you problem solve this issue or emotionally cope? That simplicity focuses your response and again externalises and rationalises your thinking.
- Ask for help. Coaching, be that for a sport or a job, helps provide another perspective about what you want to achieve and how best to get there.

- And remember, when things get tough, the tough-minded phone a friend.

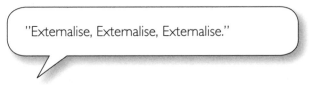

"Externalise, Externalise, Externalise."

USEFUL THINKING

The next stage in your journey to a Willpower Mindset is to move on from reality thinking to useful thinking.

An ability to modify and be in charge of your thinking allows you to react more effectively and appropriately to events in your life. There is a place for unhappiness and upset, but at some stage you are ready to move on, and *useful thinking* speeds up that process and means that you can modify these automatic thoughts to move purposefully towards solutions to your problems.

Table 4.2 lists examples of *faulty thinking* which use negative, unhelpful language in a situation like a presentation or an interview. *Less effective thinking* is marginally better, as you are telling yourself to stop, but the negative language counteracts that advice. *Useful thinking,* on the other hand, is not excessively positive, but instead mentions "coping", "success next time" and "beginning to make progress".

The language we use in our heads, about ourselves, we would probably never use towards others. Well, not if we want to keep our friends. We happily use imprecations like "you stupid idiot", "you unmitigated fool" and worse about ourselves. We beat ourselves up. Compare the sound of "I'm so nervous I've blown it" with "I'm usually calm and confident, I can cope with it". The former agitates, the latter soothes.

Think of examples of your own faulty thoughts, past or present, then change the language to more useful thinking. Note the difference in how these new thoughts can change the way you feel. Don't bother with the less effective thinking column. It is not good to learn the wrong or less effective way of doing things. Go straight for success and mastery.

Remember to change your faulty thinking to useful thinking using positive words, not "I will not be disorganised" but "I am usually organised and I will be again if I spend a day sorting myself out".

TABLE 4.2 Faulty, Less Effective and Useful Thinking Examples

FAULTY THINKING	LESS EFFECTIVE THINKING	USEFUL THINKING
I'm so nervous I've blown it!	Don't get anxious! You'll blow it!	I am usually calm and confident – I can cope with it.
I was a total failure – Everyone will think I'm an idiot.	I wasn't a total failure. Maybe next time.	Most of it was okay. I'll know what to do next time.
I didn't get anything I wanted. I'll never do any better.	I didn't get all I wanted. I should have done it better.	I didn't get everything I wanted, but I did it and that's really positive. I'm making progress.

To move your thinking towards the right-hand column, ask yourself, is this situation all bad or are there some positive aspects which could be worked upon? If your sense of humour is based on put downs and negatives, work hard to find an alternative. It might be clever, but ultimately it upsets and undermines you and others' views of you.

There are positives in almost any situation, even the most challenging. Often this is only in retrospect, but they are there nonetheless. It is worth remembering these positives when the next crisis happens.

Actions to Achieve Useful Thinking
- Deal in specifics not generalities. Nothing is ever all bad. Look for the positives.
- Make sure your internal dialogue uses positive language.
- How might you have coped in the past?
- What can you do right now to make things better?
- Focus on outcomes.
- Relax, worrying makes you negative.

ACHIEVE A WILLPOWER MINDSET

Acquire a Growth Mindset
You may have heard about a Growth Mindset before, but many people might not understand it fully. *Carol Dweck* is a professor at Stanford

University and author of *Mindset: The New Psychology of Success*. She says:

> *"As soon as a growth mindset became a desirable thing to have, many people started saying they had it. If they were open minded and flexible, they said they had a growth mindset. If they were kind to people, they said they had a growth mindset. A growth mindset is not something you declare, it's a really difficult journey you take over a long period of time."*

The Difference Between Fixed and Growth Mindsets?

A *fixed mindset* says that your basic qualities (like intelligence) are set. You have what you have and that's all you're getting.

A *growth mindset* is a belief that your abilities can be improved through effort and this means you can learn and change and that effort pays off.

With a fixed mindset, you believe talents, abilities and intelligence are fixed traits. This leads to thinking like "If I do this will I look smart? Will I feel smart? Will people think I'm talented or not?"

When you are in a growth mindset, you look at your talent and abilities as things that can be developed through hard work, good strategies, or with input from others. You are much more willing to jump in, embark on a challenge and cope with the hurdles because you're not seeing everything as reflecting on how clever you are.

Carol Dweck says "When people have a fixed mindset and they don't do well at something immediately, they quit. If you don't believe you can really improve, why keep trying?"

I have to admit to a fixed mindset as a child. When I went to ballet classes, I saw other children do remarkable things with their limbs and my immediate thoughts were "I can't do that. I'll never be able to do that." It never occurred to me, never crossed my mind, to practise. Perhaps I would never be quite as good as they were, but I could have become better. The result was that eventually I gave up ballet and took up singing, where I felt I had a natural aptitude. Singing I did work on, and I ended up singing in Scottish Opera's Chorus.

It took me a long time, into my 20s, to realise you could work on things and gradually improve. Sport, gym, book writing! When you have a growth mindset, opportunities can be grasped, and it is important that this is developed for willpower and your Willpower Challenge.

Julie Ashmore, the North and South Poles adventurer we met earlier in this book, is a great example of someone with a growth mindset.

"My willpower is about having the confidence and mindset to know that I can and will finish. Willpower definitely grows the more you achieve the little things despite adversity. And the more I believe I'll gain more confidence as I proceed, then the more I know I can continue on increasingly challenging roads to achieve even bigger things. So willpower grows over time.

On the other hand, I think the opposite is true as well, that if you get into a habit of quitting, then I think it's easy to say, well I've just not got good willpower. You can train yourself and others to keep building on willpower starting with small things and keep going."

Like Julie, when people are in a growth mindset, they are keen to take on challenging tasks. They overcome failures or obstacles rather than giving up. They are more inspired by people who are better than they are, instead of being intimidated and discouraged.

One of the most intriguing things Carol Dweck discovered was that there isn't a strong relationship between parents' mindsets and their kids'. Many parents may have a growth mindset, but it's not visible. Parents need to find out what is going on with their children's mindset and why they might opt out or into challenges. They need to focus on a child's hard work, their improvement, instead of just rewarding the child's ability or success.

Carol's Tips for Encouraging a Growth Mindset in your Children:
Compliment effort Don't praise ability or intelligence as that promotes a fixed mindset. Compliment effort, process and choices.

Attribute success to effort You can be happy when your kid succeeds, but attribute it to effort.

Respond positively to failure They need to know that failure isn't bad, it's a tool for improving.

Set goals Don't just say "try hard".

Teach a growth mindset in all areas of life There will always be areas where they can improve with hard work.

Talk to your kids about your own growth mindset efforts Practise it yourself and share your results.

Visualising Success
Visualisation is so much more of a powerful tool than most of us realise. If we visualise a successful outcome, then it is much more likely to happen as we

are drawn to that conclusion. It is mental programming. Sadly, the opposite is also true. If we visualise a negative outcome, then it is also more likely to happen. This is not a simplistic "alternative" philosophy but quite a complex chaining of beliefs and events which culminates in a self-fulfilling prophecy.

The trick with visualisation is to imagine good outcomes as vividly as possible and all the steps to success. Think of your mind's eye as a television screen where you are increasing the colour and brightness controls to gain maximum impact. In a day-dreaming moment at a bus stop, coffee break or journey home, imagine successful solutions or positive possibilities to any issue or problem you might have. This raises your awareness and alerts you to opportunities. A bit like when you buy a red car and that day you become aware of vast numbers of red cars inhabiting the roads of Britain. Our perceptions are heightened and honed towards our goals and desires. Another interesting aspect is that our brains don't register the difference between the outside world of action and what we visualise with our eyes shut. The programming is the same.

Visualising success is a major tool in your armoury to combat negative predictions and it can change your whole style of thinking to be more solution focused.

Go to the end of Part Two to find the instructions for visualisation or go to www.rostaylorcompany.com/relaxation to download the audio link to your phone or tablet.

The Power of Visualisation
An example of the power of visualisation for a positive mindset is from *Jamie Baker*, a former British tennis star now tennis television pundit.

> *"At the age of 13 I was diagnosed with osteocondritis disecans which is a degenerative knee condition. I was told I may never play again and ended up not playing for a year.*
>
> *I was determined the injury wasn't going to beat me and I was always looking for things to do that would make the most of my time off. I had already built a strong relationship with a sports psychologist. He has always been a big believer in the power of mental rehearsal and we decided that I would give it a go.*
>
> *He came up with exercises and ideas that would allow my mind to think I was training and playing tennis matches during my time off.*

He came up with audio scripts that I would listen to and we had matches and training sessions. I would take myself to a quiet place, shut my eyes, and listen to the scene being set for me – the court, the ball, the temperature, the noises, the score, winning and losing. Usually the scripts were about 20/30 minutes as any longer was a challenge to keep the appropriate level of concentration.

Aside from the audio scripts I would also get in front of a mirror and shadow play points and different shots. Sounds crazy but it worked. The other major exercise was distributing tennis balls around the house just so that the ball was still a major part of my life and it was always there if I wanted to pick it up, throw it, shadow a serve, anything. I even slept with one beside me in bed!

After a year off, although my body was weaker and out of shape, when I first came back on court, I can honestly say that in terms of hitting the tennis balls it felt like I had never been away from the court. I was genuinely shocked how well I played when I returned and I put it all down to the daily imagery I was doing."

Self-Esteem

Finally, complete the Self-Esteem Checklist here and refer to it if you encounter any setbacks and want a spirit lift. Complete it quickly and, if you can get to the end with all questions answered, then your self-esteem is high. If you falter and can't finish the list, then return to the *Reality thinking* section of the book and benchmark your skills and talents with friends and colleagues to obtain realistic feedback about your strengths.

View this checklist as a work in progress and perhaps your next Willpower Challenge.

We all have a unique contribution. It does not mean we are puffed up with arrogance if we know what we are good at. It is a realistic appraisal. A friend sent me this quote last night as I was completing this part of the book. I loved it and hope you do too:

> "Today you are You, that is truer than true. There is no one alive who is Youer than You."
>
> —Dr Seuss

The Self-Esteem Checklist

1. One thing I like about myself is _____
2. One thing others like about me is _____
3. One thing I do very well is _____
4. A recent problem I've handled very well is _____.
5. When I'm at my best I _____
6. I'm glad that I _____
7. Those who know me are glad that I _____
8. A compliment that has been paid to me recently is _____
9. A value that I try hard to put into practice is _____
10. An example of my caring about others is _____
11. People can count on me to _____
12. They said I did a good job when I _____
13. Something I'm handling better this year than last is _____
14. One thing that I've overcome is _____
15. A good example of my ability to manage my life is _____
16. I'm best with people when _____
17. A recent temptation that I managed to overcome was _____
18. I pleasantly surprised myself when I _____
19. I think that I have the courage to _____
20. If I had to say one good thing about myself I'd say that I _____
21. One way I successfully control my emotions is _____
22. One way in which I am very dependable is _____

If you love what you do, know your strengths but have a desire to improve and learn, are optimistic in the face of adversity, think usefully in a crisis, visualise success constantly and have a positive view of yourself, then congratulations, you are employing a Willpower Mindset.

The last word comes from *Iain Somerside*, a GB rowing coach who runs a high performance rowing programme for juniors at Glasgow Schools Rowing Club. The programme is widely regarded as one of the top junior performance programmes in Great Britain. Last year, six of his athletes represented Great Britain and two of them won World Championships. This year he has a further six athletes hoping to represent Great Britain. I asked him if young rowing athletes have innate ability, or whether a willpower mindset can replace a lack of natural talent. Here is what he says:

"I believe more in nurture than nature in learning and development. I know what can be achieved in developing talent through the 10 000-hour rule and the principles of deep practice. Deep practice can be used to develop skills and train the mind and in a sport such as rowing, having the correct mindset is key.

One of the things I ask my athletes at Hard Camp (a six-day intensive training camp at the start of each season) is how much of what they need to win will be technical, how much down to training and how much down to mindset.

The answers are usually 30% technical, 50% training and 20% mental. Now there is not a right or wrong answer, but by the end of Hard Camp we ask the same question again and the results have changed. Typically, they now say 20% technical, 40% training and 40% mindset. After winning the World Rowing Championships last year, Josh Armstrong told me it was 80% mental 10% technical and 10% training. His rationale is that without the correct mindset you are unable to achieve the technical ability or complete the training required to be World Champion. In that I totally agree with him.

Like any other skill, a willpower mindset can be trained, but I believe that the basis for developing this skill is the confidence that comes from knowing that you have followed the training process, have developed armour to push yourself beyond what is normally expected of the body and certainly beyond what youngsters are normally capable of achieving.

Rowing as a sport suits large athletes who have the correct physique, but our programme has proved that small athletes can achieve as much as larger athletes through sheer determination and mental toughness. A typical female rower will be six feet tall and 80 kg but we have two junior women athletes at 5' 4" and 65 kg yet they can beat the larger rowers. While you can argue that they may have better boat moving skills, much of what they achieve is because they have the correct mindset. A mindset that they have developed over the past four years and which allows them to deliver World Class performances.

I had one very small athlete who only had one and a half lungs due to a birth defect and throughout his life everyone had told him that he would not achieve anything. He was too small and not physically robust, but he was determined to prove them wrong. He was in our programme for two years and was one of the top junior scullers in the country, despite his size. The system is geared towards looking for big people and when a small person comes along and they try to beat the system they get tested more robustly than anyone else. Every time he competed he became more determined to win, and that made him stronger. If there had been a dog running past that day, he would have competed against the dog! This small guy succeeded and was in the Quadruple Scull that won the Junior World Championship last year.

Willpower is the ability to take a step into the unknown even when your brain is sending cautionary messages to your body that you should not do this. It may hurt, it may not end and it could be worse than you imagine. Top athletes override these messages and can take that step into the unknown. This is when they achieve the things that mere mortals see as extraordinary."

"The power of a positive mindset makes willpower limitless."

REMINDERS

- Identify any negative thinking.
- Know if you are an optimist or a pessimist and take action.
- Become a researcher in your life and embrace reality thinking to understand your strengths.
- Use useful thinking to change your inner dialogue to become positive.
- Utilise a growth mindset which views life as a learning experience that never ends, visualise success in all aspects of your life and also work towards high self-esteem to achieve a willpower mindset.

You are Now Ready to Go Forward Purposefully with your Willpower Challenges:

- You understand willpower.
- You have your goals in place and a fail-proof plan.
- You know all about habits and how to replace old with new.
- You have a willpower mindset.

I think a pat on the back is in order: well done – it's been quite a journey.

Now, if your Willpower Challenge or Challenges are focused on work, then read Part Five: Willpower and Work.

PART FIVE

Willpower and Work

Why should there be a separate chapter for the exercising of willpower at work? Surely the same precepts are in play? Well, the answer is yes and no.

I asked a variety of successful leaders, ones from corporate life and others who have their own businesses, how willpower might have played a part in their success. Let's start with some thoughts from *Sir Richard Greenbury*. I interviewed him many years ago, just before he left Marks and Spencer, and asked him about his success and how he would advise young aspiring leaders.

> *"I had to learn to develop and communicate a consistent vision and so I had to have a very clear idea of where the business was going. I also learned to acquire patience. Not everyone thinks in the same way or at the same pace.*
>
> *During bad patches I can begin to question my decisions, but I have learned not to let that dominate my thinking.*
>
> *You need to grab opportunities if you want to get ahead. And if you achieve them then you will be promoted. Do not be frightened of the 'big jobs' or the international assignments. That broadening is very important for success.*
>
> *Work on having the desire to go to the next rung of the promotional ladder, not an overriding desire to get to the top. Then you will make decisions that will help the business first. It's all about the business – not just **your** willpower, **your** ambition. If you focus on the latter, those around you will find a way to bring you down."*

I have an abiding memory of him after our interview calling out as I walked down Baker Street urging me not to write one of these books about selfish goal planning to get you to the top. "It's all about the business" he shouted.

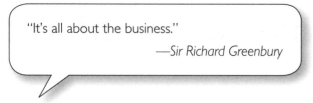

"It's all about the business."

—*Sir Richard Greenbury*

So willpower at work is not all about you, and therein lies the difference. Of course you need grit and determination, but to be successful you have to take others with you. Success at work is rarely a solo endeavour.

We have arrived at the final chapter now, and if you have been progressing through each part then a reminder of what has been learned about Willpower is in order.

Willpower is:
- The ability to delay gratification, resisting short-term temptations in order to meet long-term goals.
- Your frontal lobe's capacity to override an unwanted thought, feeling or impulse.
- The ability to employ a rational cognitive system of behaviour rather than an emotional one.
- Conscious, effortful regulation of yourself by yourself.
- The turning by repetition of willpower behaviour into habit.
- A mindset which overcomes challenges and willpower depletion.

All of the above are essential in the workplace but not *sufficient* for achievement, so I have proposed the *Three S's* to help your willpower at work.

The Three S's of Willpower at Work

1. **Self-awareness.**

2. **Skills.**

3. **Self-preservation.**

Unless you are a sole trader (and even then you will have some interaction with customers, virtual or otherwise) you will have to include others in your plans. To progress, you may have to become a leader, and so the knowledge that comes from *self-awareness* will be crucial to your success.

Willpower, with its ingredients of grit and determination, will get you only so far as there are some important work *skills* that, if adopted and practised to become part of your work routine, will help you climb the business ladder.

Self-preservation is important as you become more successful with a potentially complex and stressful existence. These are personal habits that are conducive to positive outcomes at work.

SELF-AWARENESS

Self-awareness is having a clear perception of your personality, including strengths, weaknesses, thoughts, beliefs, motivation and emotions. Self-awareness allows you also to understand other people, how they perceive you, your attitude and your responses to them. The importance of knowing yourself is absolutely crucial to achieving a happy home life and a successful work life. Unfortunately, many people are steered into lifestyles and careers that are not suited to their true aptitudes and desires. When we are impressionable and under the control of others, notably our parents and teachers, we are likely to be directed where they want us to go – not into the things that really match our skills and truly excite us. Indeed, a part of our culture in the past has been an acceptance that work is not meant to be enjoyed but exists as a means to an end: a way of spending 48 weeks of the year earning sufficient money to enjoy the remaining 4. It doesn't have to be like that.

If you know what you're good at, then you can move sideways, upwards or indeed away to pursue something better.

Let's start your self-awareness journey with an overview of your life and work with the Imagine Exercise. If you would like to draw the four sections, even better, as visual images stay with us.

Imagine Exercise
1. *Where you have come from in your life and career.* For example, family situation, background, education, job history.
2. *Where you are now in your career at work.* For example, type of work, indoor/outdoor, position, office.

3. *Where you want to be in your career at work.* For example, position, responsibility, remuneration, teamwork, job satisfaction.
4. *What you need to do to get there.* For example, development, experiences, networking, interviews, people skills.

When I first completed this exercise, I drew each of the four sections and within the year I had achieved all the goals I had set myself in life as well as career – and, believe me, drawing is not one of my strengths.

With this overview of your life and work firmly in mind, as well as a reminder of the nature of willpower above, I would like you to think about how you apply willpower at work.

The Willpower at Work Scale

Table 5.1 lists a number of statements in the Willpower at Work Scale that may or may not apply to you. For an accurate score, think of how you compare to most people – not just the people you know well, but people in general. There are no right or wrong answers, so just answer honestly!

Tick the relevant box in the following Willpower at Work Scale.

TABLE 5.1 Willpower at Work Scale

1. I have overcome setbacks at work to deliver an important challenge	
Very much like me	
Mostly like me	
Not much like me	
Not like me at all	
2. I never seem to get sufficient sleep to work energetically every day	
Very much like me	
Mostly like me	
Not much like me	
Not like me at all	
3. I tend to move from job to job	
Very much like me	
Mostly like me	
Not much like me	
Not like me at all	

4. I motivate others to succeed	
Very much like me	
Mostly like me	
Not much like me	
Not like me at all	
5. I start a project well but then I lose enthusiasm	
Very much like me	
Mostly like me	
Not much like me	
Not like me at all	
6. I remain cool in a crisis	
Very much like me	
Mostly like me	
Not much like me	
Not like me at all	
7. I am a hard worker	
Very much like me	
Mostly like me	
Not much like me	
Not like me at all	
8. I often set goals but struggle to get there	
Very much like me	
Mostly like me	
Not much like me	
Not like me at all	
9. I tend to get stressed at work	
Very much like me	
Mostly like me	
Not much like me	
Not like me at all	

(Continued)

10. I finish whatever I start

Very much like me	
Mostly like me	
Not much like me	
Not like me at all	

11. I'm pretty cynical about change programmes at work

Very much like me	
Mostly like me	
Not much like me	
Not like me at all	

12. I have achieved a business goal that took years of work

Very much like me	
Mostly like me	
Not much like me	
Not like me at all	

13. I get distracted easily at work

Very much like me	
Mostly like me	
Not much like me	
Not like me at all	

14. I really enjoy a new workplace challenge

Very much like me	
Mostly like me	
Not much like me	
Not like me at all	

Scoring

1. For questions 1, 4, 6, 7, 10, 12 and 14 assign the following points:
    3 = Very much like me
    2 = Mostly like me
    1 = Not much like me
    0 = Not like me at all

2. For questions 2, 3, 5, 8, 9, 11 and 13 assign the following points:
    0 = Very much like me
    1 = Mostly like me
    2 = Not much like me
    3 = Not like me at all

The maximum score is 42 with a minimum of 0. See where your score fits in with the scoring key.

Scoring Key

A *0* to *10* score means that you tend to be unfocused with few goals and challenges in your life. You start but don't finish tasks and have little willpower to effect change. You would enjoy increased success if you employed more willpower to establish routines at work. You may also feel the stress of being chaotic with your workload. Working towards goals and managing distractions should be added to your Willpower Challenge.

An *11* to *21* score suggests that you may occasionally complete tasks and may reach some of your goals, but not systematically. Reminding yourself to use willpower every day would help you to deliver to deadlines more effectively. Add these to your Willpower Challenge.

A *21* to *31* score reveals some willpower but it is not consistent. Your willpower is not quite at the stage of establishing routines which have become second nature at work. Remember the three-week rule to establish a new behaviour and another nine to create a habit. Add these routines to your Willpower Challenge

A *32* to *42* score is excellent, revealing consistent willpower at work. If your score is nearer 32 than 42, review your scores to discover which areas of work might require your focus to achieve a perfect score. Might it be relaxation, having more focus, goal planning or taking others with you? If so, add these to your Willpower Challenge.

Feedback at Work

To receive feedback from your boss, colleagues or team, you might have undergone a 360° assessment. As a coach, I find this process invaluable when helping clients to achieve their potential as it helps to set personal and work goals for change. You don't have to wait for your organisation to initiate a 360°, however. I have listed three killer questions below that you can email to your boss, colleagues and team asking for honest feedback to help you achieve self-awareness and progress in your career.

Three Killer Questions
1.   Three things you would like me to stop doing.
2.   Three things you would like me to continue doing.
3.   Three things you would like me to start doing.

A desire for feedback is central to a growth mindset and therefore to willpower at work. I have always found feedback respondents to be very balanced in their replies, so don't be upset by their perceptions or dismissive of the information. Others' perceptions are facts, so although your behaviour may not have been premeditated, those around you have a legitimate view. This information is like gold dust and should be treated with reverence and acted upon.

SKILLS FOR BUSINESS SUCCESS

A number of years ago, I interviewed 80 Chief Executives from the FTSE 200 to discover what they thought had made them successful. I used checklists, psychometrics and an open-ended interview and collated all the results to produce a list of skills for success. I will share these skills with you here, with some activities to achieve mastery.

Let me introduce you to *Gordon Baker*, CEO of JMP Consulting, specialists in transport planning and engineering recently acquired by SYSTRA Group. He shared some insights with me about what he felt were the limitations of willpower at work.

> *"I think that the way in which you use willpower is highly influenced by the experience you have as you grow up and mature. So something that you might have been absolutely determined to see through at the age of 25, could mean that by the time you're 40, you might not do in exactly the same way but you could still be as determined. At 40, you should lead more by listening to what your team are saying to help you succeed . . . but you're still determined to succeed.*
>
> *Stubbornness is part of willpower and our family have it in spades, but it can be completely counter-productive as a leader. If you're determined that you're right and everybody else is wrong, and actually it turns out you were wrong, you often don't discover this until you've lost a million pounds. And all because you've just been so determined to drive something through. So skills of inclusion, listening to your team and advisors, coaching rather than telling become important when you are a leader. You need skills."*

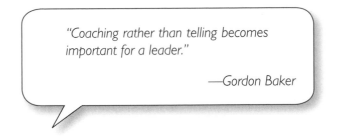

"Coaching rather than telling becomes important for a leader."

—*Gordon Baker*

So there you have it – you need skills in addition to sheer willpower to achieve your goals at work; but of course establishing these skills as part of your behavioural repertoire requires willpower. Here are six skills suggested by our group of 80 CEOs which helped them and can now enhance your success.

Six Skills to Achieve Success
1. Relate.
2. Problem solve.
3. Deliver the goods.
4. Want to win.
5. Be confident.
6. Love change.

1. Relate

Our survey of leaders revealed that they prize their ability to relate with a wide variety of people. Leaders have learned to stay close to their customers and their employees. They take time to relate to other people and are empathetic, communicative and supportive. They also handle difficult people skillfully and value a happy domestic life.

Male CEOs in our sample mentioned managing relationships at home as an essential skill. When life was not harmonious at home they felt distracted from their businesses. And they should know, as many were on their third or fourth wives. Female CEOs said relationships at home didn't really impinge on work as they had to do everything domestically anyway. Whoops.

A CEO of a prominent Building Society claimed that relationships were paramount at work. He commented that as CEO he had learned to speak to everyone in the company and, if he finished work early, he would just walk around and chat. He loved coaching staff throughout his career. He said: "They become more proficient, I get promoted. It's a win-win for all of us." He added that to be successful you require the skills to deal with your customers as well as influencing upwards to get your ideas taken on board.

Organisations are comprised of individuals, a fact which seems astoundingly obvious but is often ignored – as if organisational culture were a separate entity, unrelated to the people involved. Creating a culture of respect needs to be established from the top. The board or top team has to model "caring" behaviour consistently to everyone at all times. This consistency is crucial: if you announce a cultural vision or mission of employee engagement you can bet your bottom dollar everyone is on high alert for sins of omission. Review Table 5.2, the Caring Versus Blaming Culture, with your organisation in mind. On which side of the cultural equation do they lie?

TABLE 5.2 The Caring Versus Blaming Culture

CARING	BLAMING
I like people	I find people wanting
I compliment people	I discover faults
I do not judge	I judge constantly
I can only change myself	Other people should do what is expected of them
I allow others to be equals no matter who they are	Few people deserve my respect
I listen to others' ideas	There is a right and wrong way of looking at things
I allow others to be right	I am invariably right
I assume responsibility for what goes wrong	I blame others for anything that goes wrong

To move away from a blame culture, I am suggesting two major skills: how to provide feedback and how to reward good performance.

The Power of Small Wins

I met Teresa Amabile, Harvard Professor, in Atlanta, where she was discussing her latest book *The Progress Principle*. She had asked over 200 workers from 7 companies to keep a daily diary of events, feelings and actions over 4 months. The results were remarkable.

She discovered that, despite not asking her research group, they spontaneously mentioned coming up with ideas on days when they were happy. Workplace happiness was recorded in diaries when a leader provided positive feedback on progress. There was even a carryover effect lasting up to two days. A good mood has a lasting effect, generating a greater variety of thinking, and this led to new ideas at work.

Also, when new ideas were respected and rewarded by leaders – even if they turned out not to work – then creativity increased. Support from their leaders was an essential component in their workplace performance. Where there was conflict and competition at the top, creativity was reduced.

Internal or "intrinsic" motivation was a major factor too, with those who enjoyed the challenge of their work being more creative. Where there were promises of rewards, fear of poor evaluations or competitiveness, then the opposite was true. They were less effective performers. So "worker of the month" schemes actually undermined creativity.

So did the leaders in Teresa's study understand the power of providing feedback on progress or, as she calls, it "the power of small wins"? They did not. When asked what leadership skills made the most difference to workforce performance, they rated progress feedback at the *bottom* of the list. Small things really do make a big difference.

Related to Teresa Amabile's research was a study carried out by Christine Porath and Amir Erez reported in the *British Psychological Society Journal* in July 2011. This study focused on rudeness. The discovery was that even if the recipient of the rude behaviour did not embark on retribution or retaliation, performance plummeted on measures of cognitive and creative tasks. Even those standing by and just witnessing the rudeness were affected. When disrespected, people shut down or use their thought processes to make sense of the rude behaviour and stop working.

> "Disrespected people shut down and stop working."

For those who merely witnessed the rudeness, they performed 20% worse on an anagram test and produced 30% fewer ideas when brainstorming than a control group. Oswald and Parnes, the originators of brainstorming, always suggested that the suspension of judgement and criticism during brainstorming created more ideas – and this is upheld here. Criticism when it is directed at your own ideas can so easily be experienced as a personal slight and then you close down.

So how should you criticise without causing offence? There's an app for that.

Skills for Feedback

When giving feedback, never indulge in put downs. Use *P.P.C.O.* Remember: if you put people or their ideas down you will never get any more suggestions again and you will certainly undermine any prospect of a culture of respect. Become skilled at feedback with P.P.C.O.

So the way P.P.C.O. works is that instead of jumping in to list your criticisms, justified or not, you control that impulse and look for some good and some potential in what is offered. Only then do you air your concerns about the idea. This can open up options for overcoming your concerns which you can proceed to discuss.

Plusses In response to any idea or suggestion from anyone anywhere at any time always mention what is good about it. This reduces defensiveness in the listener, but it is also a great Willpower Challenge in the person providing feedback to first look at all times for the positives.

Potential Next, mention where this idea could be taken, how it might be useful. Remember: there is no such thing as a bad idea, just the wrong time for it.

Concerns Now talk about any concerns you might have, what are the downsides.

Overcoming concerns Next, both of you can look at options to overcome concerns – perhaps brainstorming the upsides of the downsides.

I had a colleague who, when I called from some far flung part of the world with a new idea, would immediately exclaim "what a load of rubbish – it will never work" before I had finished the sentence. I decided to share P.P.C.O. with him before our relationship deteriorated further, and I can now hear him hesitating as he searches for some kind of worth in my ideas. P.P.C.O. has saved our working relationship.

Of course you then require willpower to catch yourself being negative, critical or cynical at all times, and that can be challenging if you have indulged in a lifetime of put downs to make yourself feel superior. Take three weeks to establish the new behaviour, and another nine of repetition to turn being positive into a habit.

Eva was a brilliant young scientist I was coaching in Switzerland who, in recognition of her talent, was promoted to team leader. She had to cope with her new job as well as being a wife and mother to two young children. She seemed to accommodate this with aplomb. However, at team meetings when anyone suggested that she do things differently or her team take on increased responsibilities, she became infuriated and obstinate, stubbornly refusing to see any positives in suggestions.

After three top team meetings with her resistance pervading each, she was fast becoming known as "difficult". She cleverly included her meeting behaviour as a focus for coaching. What transpired after discussion was that she was understandably under pressure with keeping everything together and, instead of finding additional ways of delegating her work, she resisted all new ideas. So after a chat with her team she embarked on the P.P.C.O. model of feedback at top team meetings. The results were immediate as everyone was wowed by her new accommodating behaviour. This didn't mean she was a pushover, as there were still duties she wanted to resist for her and the team, but voicing her concerns in a cool rational way, not a hot and emotional one, allowed discussion and problem solving. On my next visit three months later she commented that the feedback model was now a habit. P.P.C.O. works.

James, a very intelligent young lawyer in a City of London Law Office, was referred by the senior partner to become more skilled as leader so that he could become a partner in the firm. Psychometrics and a 360° survey revealed that he was disliked by his peers and team as he used his intellect as a blunt instrument to put others down. No one was ever as good a lawyer; certainly no one could be as clever. We discussed the nature of leadership combined with a culture of respect and I suggested P.P.C.O. He looked astonished at the mere consideration of looking for positives in others' suggestions and, despite a reminder of his 360° feedback, he chose to cling to his intellectual superiority. He was refused promotion.

Recognition of small wins and skilled feedback will keep you in the caring side of the cultural equation.

2. Problem Solve

Your business success depends on you being the person who stays constructive and creative when the going is tough. You need to believe that there is always a way through, even when those around you have given up.

Meet *Justine Roberts* who, when pregnant in 2000, set up the website Mumsnet which offers solutions to parenting problems. For the first five years it was unprofitable, but now with over 50 million page views a month it turns over four million pounds from advertising. She talked to us about problem solving and willpower.

> *"I do enjoy a challenge and the thing I probably enjoy doing more than anything is working out solutions to problems. And that can take many forms: it can be the problem of how to maintain an entrepreneurial start-up environment in a growing business.*
>
> *Well, I've never really analysed it, but I think what everyone enjoys about problem solving is feeling that you've solved the problem and taken people with you. I like the analytical challenge of doing the job I do. It's very data led, there's a lot of analysis. It's great to have a digital product where you have constant real time data, I like that, I like being able to use that to engineer solutions.*
>
> *I have a lot of infrastructure now and a lot of support and a lot of good people, so it's a different kind of challenge really. The challenge is running and managing a small to medium sized business with 120 employees which is different. But also I find it incredibly stimulating and challenging, so I'm still up for it basically.*
>
> *Mumsnet and its purpose hasn't deviated since it started. Obviously there have been many twists and turns in terms of business planning, but in terms of actually what it's for, why we are doing this, it's exactly the same message as it was 16 years ago. Mumsnet is about making parents' lives easier and solving their problems. The idea is that by pooling the wisdom of the crowd, you can make parents' lives easier. And not just advice but support as well. And simply the knowledge that you're not alone, that other people have been there and survived.*
>
> *I genuinely think that there is something about truth on Mumsnet. People are anonymous, so being able to share situations honestly and benefit from other people's input, to know they've gone through*

these same challenges, that you're not alone. Whatever it is that's bothering you, relationships, family life, or work, it's just a great idea that other people have dealt with similar situations and can help.

As for willpower, well I think it's putting off immediate gratification. That's the test. It's not doing what in the short term gives you pleasure in favour of long-term benefit. I'm also just bloody-minded and I don't listen to naysayers."

So Justine Roberts is a very successful problem solver in the business of parental problems. My 80 CEOs ranked problem solving at the top of their list of skills and many mentioned that they had volunteered to sort out issues at work when no one else stepped up and – when they became successful – were jettisoned to the top.

A skill that I would rate as essential in this arena is Mind Mapping.

Mind Mapping

Mind Maps can help an individual or team to identify speedily the overall concept of an issue, as you can see the way that pieces of information fit together (see Figure 5.1). Mind Mapping can also help you remember information as it is in a format that your mind finds easy to recall. Wonderful for presentations! I am not sure that I would have been able to speak at so many conferences and seminars if Mind Mapping had been unavailable as a tool.

Mind Maps were popularised by Tony Buzan and because Mind Maps are more compact than conventional notes, just taking up one side of paper, you can make associations more easily and generate new ideas. If you find out more information after you have drawn a Mind Map, then you can just add it to a branch with little disruption. When I think back to working in a linear structure with arrows all over the place, adding new ideas as they came to me, I realised it was messy – leading to befuddled thinking.

In addition, Mind Mapping helps you to break large projects or topics down into manageable chunks, so that you can plan effectively without getting overwhelmed and without forgetting something important. I have used Mind Mapping increasingly for business plans. At every meeting you can produce it and add to it if necessary. It's all on one page. Simple.

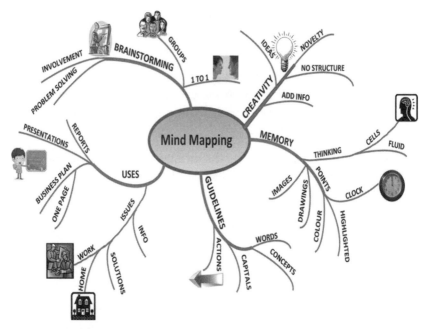

FIGURE 5.1 Sample Mind Map

Rules for Mind Mapping
1.   Put the title in the centre.
2.   Use capitals – you can see them more easily.
3.   Use lines for information connected to the centre.
4.   Use only one or two words along the lines.
5.   Use colour to identify sections and aid memory.
6.   Keep your mind free of structure.

3. Deliver the Goods
Successful people know what has to be done. And they need to achieve results. The key is the development of a results focus in which the end point is clearly understood and there is a sense of urgency in striving to get there. Once there, of course, new goals are set and the process begins again. In our survey of the characteristics of success, "needing to achieve results" was the second most highly rated item overall. Among women, it was rated as *the* most important single characteristic.

In one of the most successful motivational books of all time, *The Seven Habits of Highly Effective People*, Steven Covey emphasises the importance of differentiating between things that are important and those that are urgent. Covey suggests that we are too easily diverted by the immediate urgency of everyday things; for example, the constant need to look at emails. The price we pay for filling our days with this urgent clutter is a failure to tackle things which are important and might develop our careers and ourselves.

Prioritise
Look at all your options for next week and place them in four quadrants (see Figure 5.2):

> *Quadrant 1* contains those things that are urgent as well as business and career enhancing.
> *Quadrant 2* contains items that will be good for business and promote your career but don't *have* to be done next week.
> *Quadrant 3* represents the things that seem urgent in that they have to be done next week, but really don't deliver much in the way of business or career development.
> *Quadrant 4* items don't have much going for them; they don't have to be done yet and they don't do much for the business or indeed your career.

Now draw up a personal action plan. Each quadrant needs to be considered separately. The business and career enhancing/urgent things (quadrant 1) clearly have to go to the top of the list. If there is no time left for anything else, then that's not too much of a problem since everything you are doing is developing the business and your career in the way you want.

FIGURE 5.2 Priorities for Business and Career

However, if there is still space in the week then there is still work to do on the diary and you need to consider some of the other quadrants.

The real challenge comes in dealing with those things that would add business and career value but which do not have urgency (quadrant 2). These are the items that prey on the conscience since you know they should be done but keep postponing them. Now is the time to grasp them! Somehow they have to be scheduled, so make the decision on how and when they are to be addressed. Perhaps they are too big and too daunting, in which case break them down into manageable elements. If the problem is that they have just been postponed too long, then write them into the plan so it is clear exactly what you are going to do and when – and then commit to them.

This might then leave the rather awkward list of things that don't add to your career but still have to be done (quadrant 3). Often, these comprise the bulk of your job. They are the routine, paper-pushing activities which, at the end of the day, might be what you get paid for. This is where a bit of creativity is called for. Can these tasks be streamlined? Have you allowed them to simply fill the time available? Are you deluding yourself that they actually have to be done? Can any of them be delegated so that some of your own time is freed up? Can they be done in a different way that is career enhancing? These items are like the scrappy files that fill up your computer memory. They need to be deleted or compressed to free up space.

Finally, if you were planning to do anything which doesn't have to be done and which also does nothing for the business or you (quadrant 4), then ditch it!

Delegate
This is another quick review, a snapshot of all that you do. Here's the proposition.

DELEGATION HABITS

You are abducted to a South Sea Island for three months quite against your will but, prior to your departure, you are allowed time to list all that you do, allocate the tasks to others and suggest any training or coaching necessary for them to get the job done while you are away. There might be a few, a very few, tasks that only you can do and can wait three months to be initiated.

Review the list once you have allocated your tasks to designated others and assigned training. The million-dollar question is: why wait for abduction, why not delegate these tasks right now, with the development programmes necessary to bring people up to scratch? There are many reasons why you might want to hang onto tasks you should have delegated years ago:

• You are good at them, better than others.
• You have received accolades for fulfilling these tasks.
• What does that leave you to do? Are you making yourself redundant?

If you have been promoted and have a strategic role to play then your time should be spent thinking, researching and coordinating others' activities. Delegation must become a habit, so the 12-week rule pertains.

A good delegation habit will leave time for work priorities, career enhancing opportunities and strategic thinking.

4. Want to Win

Those at the top have a drive to become successful and see this as an objective in its own right. They enjoy winning for the sake of it and often think of business life as a game. This used to infuriate me, as clearly it's not a game to have many employees' livelihoods dependent on you. However, on reflection, I realised that the "game" concept allowed them to make rational not emotional decisions.

Charlie Mullins of Pimlico Plumbers has 350 staff, 45 apprentices and 25 million in revenue. He talks here about willpower and winning.

> *"I think willpower is something where you're prepared to get on with it. It doesn't matter how many knocks or blows you take, if you think that you're on to a winner, it's like getting back on the horse. If you think that horse is going to win you get back on that horse. Willpower is where you take all the blows and you just carry on and carry on and they're not going to beat you. You're not going to give in to people and by not giving in, I think that is willpower at work.*
>
> *Determination, I think that's a nicer word. It's like a boxer, if you get knocked over in the ring, it's quite simple — you either get up and you might win a fight, or you stay down and lose. I think you've got*

to keep on getting up and getting up and getting up until you get on top of the opposition. And I think that's willpower, never giving in.

I think I've always had willpower to win. You've got to have that in you, you've got to have that consistency of not being trod upon. Saying that, when I was a kid I was bullied and then I started boxing and it changed my outlook, so actually you can develop willpower. I think if you're taught that you don't have to be second best and if you box it's very clear that you're either a loser or a winner and if you want to win, you've got to keep going. There's nothing like having your own business, I think it's the best feeling in the world."

Celebrate Winning

Life is so hectic that one project has barely finished before another has started. Closure and the reinforcement of success is motivational. So here is an exercise for this section: write down at least six ideas to celebrate winning. Some should be personal rewards, rewarding yourself for an achievement or completion of a project, and if you work in a team, write down what you can do together to mark success.

Teresa Amabile's research shows that monetary rewards are unnecessary, but a "well done" and a team night out work a treat. I remember Raj, a group leader in a pharmaceutical company, who took his team out for a pizza and a movie on a Friday afternoon every month when they hit target. The other managers were aghast. Who had sanctioned this and what budget was used? He calmly replied that it was his idea and everyone paid for themselves. His team loved these afternoons and were motivated to hit target as soon as possible. Raj was chosen out of all the managers to be promoted to director. He made work fun.

Of all the CEOs I have interviewed, Julian Richer, CEO of Richer Sounds, was the one who understood the importance of winning and recognition. He said:

"I have always been entrepreneurial. Even at school I was selling things. But I had to realise that I couldn't do it all on my own. To grow a business, I had to learn to motivate and delegate. Once the business had grown, keeping that buzz is the challenge. I would advise any aspiring leader to learn how to motivate the people around you. Understand what drives them and reward them when they reach their targets. It sounds simple but it works. Sadly, most leaders don't do it."

5. Be Confident

Some of the CEOs in our sample maintained they were born confident, for others it had to come with the job, so the majority rated their confidence as high. This seems to be an essential requirement since they need to speak up for themselves, to argue effectively with senior colleagues and to be the focus of attention in a range of business situations. Most felt they had to look and act confident even on bad days.

It is worth mentioning that confidence is not about arrogance. That strutting, boastful, bragging behaviour is often mistaken for confidence by those who are not, but is, in fact, based on insecurity.

Confident people, comfortable in the knowledge of their talents, are relaxed and keen to listen and learn from others. They have a growth mindset. The arrogant are self-orientated, keen to hear themselves talk, and so worried they are not good enough that they have to tell everyone how good they are. All signs of a fixed mindset. Never mistake this for confidence.

Dame Stella Rimington, formerly Director General of MI5 and Non-Executive director of Marks and Spencer, BG and GKR among others, and now an author, told me:

> *"I had to learn to be confident. I was a very anxious person when younger, being sick before exams and that kind of thing. I can trace that anxiety back to my experience of air raids as a child during the war. And I had to learn to be less self-conscious and more orientated towards those I was leading. This was a gradual learning process as I achieved promotion through the ranks.*
>
> *I also had to manage risk, often on the basis of inadequate information. I had to learn to be even-tempered as I was prone to be emotional when younger. I am therefore much better at handling difficult people now and will try not to have head on confrontations.*
>
> *The press was very intrusive in a quite inappropriate way when I first became Head of MI5. What I wore and where I bought it became the focus of many an article while I was trying to focus on national security. They found out where I lived and so forced me to move from a house in which I was very comfortable. I really resented that.*

Young managers need to become self-confident and learn to work with a wide variety of people. Developing the ability to work in and through teams is an essential skill today."

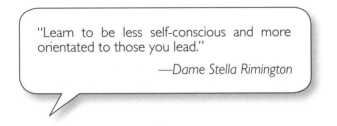

"Learn to be less self-conscious and more orientated to those you lead."

—*Dame Stella Rimington*

To rate your own confidence, complete the *Confidence Checklist* (see Table 5.3) by answering yes or no to the statements.

TABLE 5.3 Confidence Checklist

1. Do you feel comfortable talking to strangers for the first time?	
2. Do you make a good first impression?	
3. Can you enter a roomful of strangers with aplomb?	
4. Do you enjoy going to social events where you meet a range of new people?	
5. Do you find it easy to make conversation with a wide variety of people?	
6. Are you relaxed socially?	
7. Are you an enthusiastic and motivated person at work and at home?	
8. Is life fun for you?	
9. Do you have high self-esteem?	
10. Do you have a positive attitude about yourself?	
11. Do you think positively about your future?	
12. Do you focus on your successes rather than your failures?	
13. When you encounter difficulties do you problem solve?	
14. Are you generally positive about other people?	
15. Do you reward and compliment those around you?	
16. Do you handle difficult people skilfully?	

17. Do you handle your emotions well, directing them appropriately?	
18. Do you cope with conflict and resolve it?	
19. Can you speak in public with ease?	
20. Are you successful at job interviews?	
21. Do you put yourself forward for promotion?	
22. Do you see yourself becoming a leader of a group, team or company?	
23. In the past have you ever successfully changed any aspect of yourself?	
24. On a rating scale of 1 to 10 (1 = low;10 = high), how confident are you?	

Scoring

Congratulations if you achieved a score of 23 and a rating of 10 on the final scale but, if not, list any "no" answers to statements and use the list as an action plan for change.

A great Willpower Challenge might be to become more confident not just at work, but in life.

6. Love Change

When I asked 80 CEOs from the FTSE 200 whether they liked change – most people don't – they told me that not only did they love change but also saw their ability to initiate change as crucial to their success. They were often hired to bring about organisational change. Embracing change, and recognising that it is now a necessary part of business life, is an essential. But so many change programmes fail.

A change plan needs to move from a document that sits on the shelf to actions that drive change. Sadly, the majority of companies who have such plans fail to implement them fully and then don't evaluate them, so there is no learning when the next one comes along. According to *Fortune Magazine*, nine out of ten organisations fail to implement their strategic change plans for many reasons:

Reasons for Failure of Change Programmes
- 60% of organisations don't link change strategy to budgets.
- 75% of organisations don't link employee performance to a change strategy.

- 86% of business owners and managers spend less than one hour per month discussing strategies for change.
- 95% of a typical workforce doesn't understand their organisation's change strategy.

A strategic plan for change provides a business with the roadmap it needs to pursue a specific direction for change and set of performance goals. However, this is just a plan; it doesn't guarantee that the desired change is reached any more than having a roadmap guarantees the traveller arriving at the desired destination.

A strategy for change needs a process which guarantees success and one which takes into account how individuals change – because organisations are comprised of individuals.

When you think about how hard it is to implement your own Willpower Challenges, can you imagine the difficulty when you have 30, 3000, 30 000 or 300 000 plus people in an organisation which might also be scattered globally? Messages become diluted, people default, others misunderstand and nothing changes.

So let me introduce you to the Willpower Process for Organisational Change (see Figure 5.3). The first step is the C.R.E.A.T.E. Process. This has been honed over years of working with companies desiring change.

FIGURE 5.3 The Willpower Process for Organisational Change

Organisational change is for the board or top team to consider, not a company-wide competition. A global HR leader told me that his CEO had asked all the millennials to strategise where the company should focus in the future. The results lacked creativity, focus and knowledge. By all means listen to everyone in the organisation, but strategic decisions for change come from the top.

Each stage of the process is explained below.

CREATE: THE PROCESS FOR ORGANISATIONAL CHANGE

Check Goals
- What goals do you want to accomplish this year?
- What challenges do you face?
- What do you wish worked better?
- What changes are necessary to move the organisation forward?
- List all ideas, then everyone in the team chooses *one* as the focus for further discussion.

How to Choose What to Work On
- What is most important to you?
- What can you influence directly?
- What urgently requires a new look?

Without going through this process, you could end up dealing with too broad an issue or goal or indeed one imposed by the group leader and not one the group as a whole wants to achieve.

Research
The next step involves researching everything surrounding the goal or issue. Remember: you are not focusing on solutions but still concentrating on the problem. There is a strong drive in all of us to want to solve instantly rather than explore. Curb that enthusiasm at this stage.

Mind Mapping is a good technique for interrogating and displaying all the underlying issues and areas of further exploration. A group can view the whole set of circumstances and then choose which strand or strands require more research and understanding. So issues are explored to expand knowledge and understanding of the goal and then a section chosen that the majority want to delve into even further.

Examine Issues

In delving into the group's selected problem or goal, view it from all angles; for example, how to make it better, how might it look, in what ways might it be changed, what additional aspects could be considered?

Create a problem statement that encapsulates what needs to be solved. This has to be brief and focused with obvious benefits to the group. This section ensures that the problem selected is *really* the one that will make a difference.

Acquire Ideas: Brainstorm

Brainstorming has been defined as "a means of getting the largest number of ideas from a group in the shortest amount of time". Recently, however, brainstorming has received a bad press – so let's look at this technique in more detail to work out whether it is indeed relevant. I had always felt slightly irritated by brainstorming in the past. Some poor sucker was at the flip chart writing down ideas that had to be dragged from a reluctant group. It was usually at the end of a meeting when everyone wanted to go to the bar or go home.

Brainstorming suggests suspending judgement to help the flow of ideas. This is, of course, challenging if you have had 20 to 40 years of being critical and judgmental about yourself and others. So some training is required for groups to free up their imagination in order to form new connections.

Guidelines for Brainstorming
- Go for quantity not quality. Don't worry about making mistakes; just go for as many ideas as possible – the time for analysis is later.
- No judgement.
- Freewheel with thoughts and ideas. Keep momentum going with the first thing that comes into your head – the faster the pace the better.
- Make connections.
- Piggyback on others' ideas – use them as prompts.

To return to the C.R.E.A.T.E. process, stage 4 is where the group brainstorms as many ideas as they can in two minutes. Wild ideas are best as they move you far from well-trodden paths.

Once all ideas are captured on a flip chart, the group chooses the best idea. Was it a very practical choice? Or was it one of the more outrageous ideas? The latter is probably the better to pursue. It is the unusual, weird, off the wall idea which you can modify to become something do-able.

The ordinary or commonplace has probably been done before and therefore will never be groundbreaking.

Test Solutions

- How might this chosen idea be improved? How might a wild idea be tamed?
- What could the group really see themselves doing?
- Is it appropriate to the organisation?
- What reservations might the group have about implementation?

When faced with wild solutions, don't cast them away. Instead ask what might be good about them, because there may be something useful even in the most extreme ideas. Incorporate some of these good things into an interesting, more do-able, solution.

How many meetings have you been at where all attending have agreed to solutions only to disagree in the coffee room afterwards? If there are reservations, then they should be discussed openly and ways around them brainstormed before finalising actions. Thus you are much more likely to achieve compliance from the group.

Enable Actions

What are all the action steps that can be taken to implement the solution? Who will undertake to do what and by when? What responsibilities need to be allocated, funds distributed? Making sure action plans are acted upon is a major role for someone in a team. It is worth charting the journey of the original idea to the end product. It is always different.

In terms of effecting change, this is only a beginning. Let me provide you with an example. A hotel chain had received their annual figures and noticed an increase in the housekeeping budget. What many organisations do at this point is issue an edict for a 15% cut in expenditure. Tick box, move on. This one did not and asked me to facilitate a discussion with the top team to come up with some solutions for change. When we Mind Mapped the issue, what emerged as the major financial burden was laundry. Replenishment of sheets and towels had gone through the roof. Delving further, they discovered that the external laundry they used was returning everything either mangled or not theirs! At this point we brainstormed – how might the hotel get better service from the laundry? The outrageous idea chosen was to open their own. They discussed their reservations and decided to pilot the idea.

This example reveals that what the team ended with was a far cry from the start of the discussion.

PILOT

Many change ideas don't work, so piloting first allows "fast failure", as Howard Shultz of Starbucks fame has suggested. With little finance expended and a new idea trialled, what's not to like? Find an area of your organisation that's discreet, i.e. separate from others, small and willing to change. If it works, this group can become ambassadors for the desired change programme.

My Women as Leaders Programme in a pharmaceutical company was piloted with Drug Discovery first before going company wide. The results showed a 40% increase in female top promotions, and so it has proved itself for a launch worldwide.

LAUNCH

When you are ready to launch your piloted idea, ensure that the W.I.I.F.M. factors are tackled. When any change is mentioned in companies, everyone defaults to "What's in it for me?" If the answer is "nothing" then kiss goodbye to your change programme. Spell it out and be truthful. If it only enables jobs to be kept, then mention that and don't over promise. A workforce is ever vigilant to notice defaulting, especially from the top.

And be honest. I was working with Wyeth Pharmaceuticals when Pfizer arrived on the scene. Both sides talked about the "merger". Pfizer is huge, Wyeth smaller and money changed hands. It was a takeover. I can see why they might have wanted to maintain the illusion so that the good scientists remained engaged and employed, but the dishonesty was risible. I was censured for suggesting to the leaders I was training that they might want a Plan B if Pfizer rejected them. Intelligent people are not hoodwinked.

And be prepared to follow up on promises. A British company was launching a new quality programme throughout the organisation, and the leader went onstage to speak to all employees and pledged that he was personally guaranteeing results. He declaimed "I will be monitoring this change project so it won't be the last time you see me." Sadly, it was. And even worse, when the assembled looked at the launch brochure it said "quaility" not "quality". It wasn't a success . . .

COACH

Top teams naively believe, I have discovered, that if they issue a mandate for change then all staff will rush off to do their bidding. Nothing could be further from the truth. To embed change in an organisation is extremely challenging with a multitude of personal and political agendas in conflict. All leaders need to be trained in *willpower coaching skills* so that every employee knows exactly how they must change, by when, and that their performance will be monitored and rewarded.

This should be a 12-week programme for each piece or cluster of behaviour.

Leaders need to evidence the changed behaviour first as role models, then they can train others. Sharing the Willpower Habit model discussed in Part Three of the book is essential for change programmes. During the first three weeks of learning the new behaviour, a leader needs to check understanding and resolve challenges. Then repetition with reminders during meetings and one-to-ones will really cement the change.

EVALUATE

Set a review process. It is the power of feedback, of review, that helps progress. So why don't organisations do it? Stress, work overload or perhaps there is a reluctance to look failure in the eye. What might be nearer the truth is that we embellish the past and put a positive spin on errors. There are many ways of doing this. We distort our memory, deny all knowledge or blame others for our mistakes.

- Take time during each meeting to have a strategic review and monitor the change progress.
- Review if not on track. Do not live wishfully. If the actions for change are not working, close them down after three months at the latest.
- Talk openly about what the change process has taught you and avoid these pitfalls next time.

"Experience is inevitable; learning is not. No review, no learning."

Let me finish my story about the hotel and the laundry. They piloted their own laundry with a second-hand machine in a warehouse and the difference was amazing. Sparkling intact sheets and towels and at a cheaper price point. So more new machines were purchased and now they are inviting other hotel groups to use their laundry.

Another example of using the Willpower Process for Organisational Change was from a famous restaurant chain who were receiving increasingly poor feedback about service in their restaurants. Mind Mapping the issues, what they chose to work on was the fact that new recruits were not being trained to a high enough standard by chefs, sommeliers or front of house staff. Many ideas emerged from that brainstorming session, but the one they chose was to set up their own Training Academy. Cleverly, they offered it first to existing staff then to all new staff joining the organisation. After understanding the nature of willpower, the Academy training lasted three weeks for everyone to learn new restaurant behaviours, then another nine in the various restaurants in the group. To cement the new behaviours, they were mentored by existing staff who had been through the programme and, when the company reviewed feedback, it had improved exponentially.

THE WILLPOWER OF YOUR OWN BUSINESS

For some, the essence of willpower at work is starting your own business. I can certainly attest to having my Willpower Challenged constantly as I have been running my own business now for over 30 years. Take the Entrepreneur Quiz here to see if you have got what it takes.

The Entrepreneur Quiz
Instructions: Read each question in this Entrepreneur Quiz and circle one of the suggested answers. Respond by marking the answer that most accurately describes your behaviour, feeling or attitude as it actually is, not as you would like it to be, or think it should be. You must be absolutely honest with yourself in order to get a valid score.

1. Are you a self-starter?
   A. If someone helps me to get started, I can keep going.
   B. I love starting things. Nobody needs to help me get started.
   C. I will start things if I really have to.

2. How do you feel about other people?
   A. Most people irritate me.
   B. I like people. I can get along with just about anybody.
   C. I have a small group of close friends.

3. Can you lead others?
   A. I can get people to do things if I motivate them.
   B. I can get most people to go along with me without much difficulty.
   C. I usually let someone else get things moving.

4. Can you take responsibility?
   A. I take over if I have to, but I'd rather let someone else be responsible.
   B. There's always some eager beaver around waiting to show off so I let them.
   C. I like to take charge and see things through.

5. How organised are you?
   A. I like to have a plan before I start. I'm usually the one who lines things up.
   B. I plan, but life often gets in the way.
   C. I just take things as they come.

6. How hard a worker are you?
   A. I can't see that hard work gets you anywhere.
   B. I'll work hard for a time, but when I've had enough, that's it.
   C. I can keep going as long as necessary. I don't mind working long hours.

7. Can you make decisions?
   A. I can if I have plenty of time.
   B. I can make my mind up in a hurry if necessary.
   C. I don't like to be the one who decides things. I let others do that.

8. Can you wait long term for your rewards from work?
   A. I like the security of knowing when I'm going to be paid.
   B. I am happy knowing I will reap the benefits later.
   C. I'm in it for the money so I will ensure I'll get paid.

9. Can you stick with it?
   A. If I make up my mind to do something, I won't let anything stop me.
   B. If a job doesn't go smoothly, I tend to give up.
   C. I generally finish what I start.

10. Can you keep records?
   A. Records are not important. I know what needs to be done without keeping records.
   B. I can, but it's more important to get the work out than shuffle numbers.
   C. Since they are needed, I will keep records even though it's not my preference.

Scoring
Award yourself the points as indicated in the table here and then total your score.

Question	Score	Question	Score
1	a 0 b 2 c 1	6	a 0 b 1 c 2
2	a 0 b 2 c 1	7	a 1 b 2 c 0
3	a 2 b 1 c 0	8	a 0 b 2 c 1
4	a 1 b 0 c 2	9	a 2 b 0 c 1
5	a 2 b 1 c 0	10	a 0 b 1 c 2
Total		Total	
Combined total:			

Results
Score 20: Excellent. A perfect score. You are a born entrepreneur. If you are not presently running your own business you should definitely start one – the sooner the better. You are on the way to fame and fortune.

Score 15–19: Very good. You definitely have what it takes to succeed in a business of your own. Don't hesitate; your way to business success is wide open.

Score 10–14: Good. You have the qualities of a successful entrepreneur with some weak spots. Read the interpretation below to identify your deficiencies. You should be able to cover these deficiencies by either retraining yourself or hiring someone with the necessary skills.

Score 5–9: Middling. The prospects of your success in a business of your own are questionable. You have some deficiencies that might overshadow some good traits. If you still want to continue you will require more willpower. You are going to face some tough times ahead.

Score 4 and below: Not for you. Forget your dreams of being your own boss, it's not for you. You'd better keep your present job. Why bother with all the risks and hassles of starting a business?

Interpretation

What Traits and Characteristics Make a Successful Entrepreneur?
Numerous studies have been made of entrepreneurs and business managers over the years. First, consider those characteristics that seem to distinguish the person who opens a business from the person who works for someone else.

People who start their own businesses usually feel and express themselves more strongly. If you are going to risk your money and time in your own business you must have a strong feeling that you will be successful, so many are optimistic.

If you want to start your own business, you are likely to have a strong need for achievement which is an important factor in success. Someone who wouldn't think of starting a business might call you a gambler or a high risk-taker. Yet you probably don't feel that about yourself.

When a person starts and manages their own business they don't see risks; they see only factors which they can control to their advantage. If you possess these traits to some degree or another it doesn't mean you will be successful, only that you will very likely start your own business.

An entrepreneur is also a hard worker who is happy to delay gratification for future success and work hard to get to where they want to be.

Characteristics of Successful Entrepreneurs
The characteristics that appear most frequently include willpower, thinking ability, relationship skills, communication skills and technical knowledge.

Willpower is composed of responsibility, vigour, initiative, persistence and health.

Thinking ability consists of original, creative, critical, and analytical thinking.

Competency in human relations means emotional stability, sociability, good personal relations, consideration, cheerfulness, cooperation and tactfulness.

Communications skills include verbal comprehension, oral and written communications.

Technical knowledge is the comprehension of the physical process of producing goods or services.

One of the interesting results that came from interviewing 80 CEOs was that there were no differences in the skills for success mentioned by corporate leaders and entrepreneurs. Top leaders of global institutions viewed them as their own and felt very similar responsibilities to entrepreneurs.

Let's hear again from *Charlie Mullins* of Pimlico Plumbers:

> *"Just to have your own business is great. I say to people starting out – there's no better business than your own business, it's a lovely thing to have. Whether you employ one person or 1000 people, having your own business is probably one of the top 10 things in your life. To run your own business and not have people telling you what to do is wonderful. To run a successful business, I don't know how to describe it, it's the ultimate."*

Charlie is so appreciative of entrepreneurship that all his plumbers are self-employed contractors.

Self-Preservation
Manage Stress
You need to manage stress levels at work. Being under high levels of stress means your body's energy is used up in acting instinctively and making decisions based on short-term outcomes. Our prefrontal cortex loses out in the battle for our energy when high stress is involved, and we know that means a reduction of willpower.

Hans Selye, the Canadian psychologist, maintains that it takes us three months to habituate to stress in our environment, and mostly we don't notice until the stress ends or we go on holiday – when it takes days to unwind. The graph in Figure 5.4 reveals how pressure can build throughout the day if no breaks are taken. If you take work home you may be taking stress home too.

Daily Pressure Build Up—after Hans Selye

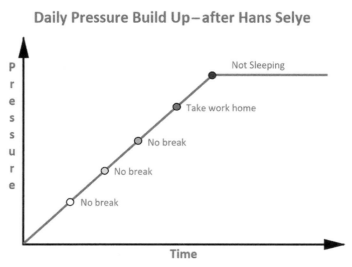

FIGURE 5.4 The Pressure Build Up

The difference between pressure and stress is when you experience symptoms such as headaches, sleeplessness, irritability or skin rashes. These are signs that your mind and body are not happy. What we do too often is ignore the signals and self-prescribe with alcohol or medication.

When we become stressed, we tend to adopt a whole plethora of unhelpful responses. We know that we should relax, take exercise, eat vitamin rich food but do we do it? Not enough. At times of stress, fast food appeals because . . . it's fast.

Seeing work as fun was a philosophy espoused by my CEO group. If you experience work as a drag the chances are you will not be successful, no matter how hard you try. Finding an area of work that is stimulating is of prime importance in achieving a key to that boardroom.

Ineffective Coping Strategies in Response to Stress
- Increased drinking.
- Increased smoking.
- Working longer hours.
- Skipping lunch.
- Withdrawal.
- Rushing about.
- Sleeping more.
- Denying there is a problem.

What's going on when we're stressed? Well, in response to stress, the adrenal glands secrete glucocorticoids, hormones that produce an array of effects in response to stress: mobilising energy into the bloodstream from storage sites in the body, increasing cardiovascular tone and delaying long-term processes in the body that are not essential during a crisis, such as feeding, digestion, growth and reproduction. Some of the actions of glucocorticoids help mediate the stress response, while other, slower, actions counteract the primary response to stress and help re-establish stability.

With short-term stress, like the experience of an interview, epinephrine mobilises energy and delivers it to muscles for the body's response. The glucocorticoid cortisol promotes energy replenishment and good cardiovascular function in case you need to flee from anything threatening.

Glucocorticoids are in fact essential for survival. They have anti-inflammatory properties through inhibition of the immune system. For example, cortisone is used as an anti-inflammatory medication; however, it cannot be used long-term as it increases susceptibility to disease due to its immune-suppressing effects. So short-term benefits are plentiful; however, in the long term there are downsides: poor attention, skewed perception, disruption to short-term memory, learning and speech. See Figure 5.5 to see what happens as a result of chronic stress on the brain.

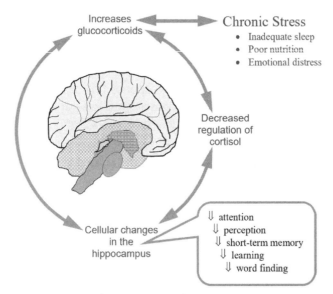

FIGURE 5.5 The Stress–Brain Loop

There are some very simple interventions you can do at work that will allow you to relax and focus on the work on hand.

The Five-Minute Break

Unions fought hard to get break pauses for employees during the working day. But what happens now is that a tea or coffee break away from your desk is frowned upon in some companies. It may not be found in job descriptions, but people just get the feeling that it is career limiting.

Of course this is foolishness. Human beings have an average concentration span of about one-and-a-half to two hours. This can be stretched if there is a crisis or a deadline to be met; however, you cannot keep expecting to work continuously in that crisis mode. If you do not take a pause, your brain takes little "micro sleeps". That means you will catch yourself looking out of the window then wondering where you were in that document; or even worse, when driving, wondering how you got there. If you do not take a break your brain will do it for you. Of course your productivity is reduced if you are in micro sleep mode. Much better to take that five-minute break to return to your desk refreshed and focused.

Set a timer on your desk and, if you are in a leadership role, be a model for good working practices. Every two hours walk around the office and chat, then focus completely in between. You will get more done.

The 15-Minute Lunch

Taking a 15-minute lunch is similar in philosophy to the five-minute break. Lunch does not have to take an hour as life is busy, and crises do happen, so an hour might be too long to be away from your desk. But you still need a break. Getting outside for a walk is preferable, but even just eating your lunch on the other side of your desk enables a concentration break and revitalises your day.

Stopping to take a few deep breaths when we feel overwhelmed or tempted can be a great start in managing stress levels and improving willpower . . . and you can do that at your desk.

Sleep

Arianna Huffington, founder of the Huffington Post, has popularised sleep. After she keeled over, breaking her jaw as a result of sleep deprivation, she has evangelised the advantages of a good night's sleep. In her book *The Sleep Revolution* she refutes popular opinion that to succeed at work you need to survive on three or four hours sleep.

We did hear that Margaret Thatcher survived on four hours, Richard Branson five and Donald Trump on the campaign trail boasted of as little as one hour a night. Arianna doesn't pull her punches as she states: "Maybe Trump's contribution to politics is a case study of the dangers of sleep deprivation. He displays the symptoms of inability to process information, impulsiveness, trouble listening to others and being prone to paranoid tendencies. Being sleep deprived is like leading while drunk."

Sleep deprivation (even just getting less than six hours a night) is a kind of chronic stress that impairs how the body and brain use energy. The prefrontal cortex is especially hard hit as it loses control over the regions of the brain that create cravings and the stress response. Basic visual and motor skills deteriorate, but higher order mental skills like problem solving, supporting others and focusing on results are compromised. Stress increases and health suffers, putting attendance at work in jeopardy. But the good news is that when the short-term sleep-deprived catch a better night's sleep, their brain scans no longer show signs of prefrontal cortex impairment.

And, if you're wondering how much sleep is enough, one of the most acclaimed sleep researchers, Daniel Kripke, found in a recent study that "people who sleep between 6.5 hours and 7.5 hours a night, live the longest, are happier and most productive". Well, that works.

Arianna suggests a 30-minute routine to wind down before going to bed, listing all tasks for the following day to get them out of your head, turn off all electronic devices and disconnect.

It also helps to learn the skills of relaxation and meditation.

Relax
Learn to relax and practise for three weeks and repeat for nine weeks to get the relaxation habit – but you will notice the difference in three weeks. Meditation has been linked to increasing reserves of willpower as well as improving attention, focus, stress management and self-awareness.

Looking at the science, the prefrontal cortex, the anterior cingulate cortex and the hippocampus all increase in density as a result of meditation. This means increased cognitive flexibility, planning and problem solving, emotional regulation, better learning and memory and more resistance to depression and anxiety. The amygdala – which governs the fight or flight response and fearful, anxious emotions – decreases in size with meditation practice. And there's more. Meditation affects the *medial prefrontal cortex* commonly known as the "*Me Centre*" because it processes information about you, thoughts about your future; and social interactions and empathy towards others.

With *meditation*, the connection of the medial prefrontal cortex and the bit of the Me Centre that's self-focused breaks down, and the connection with the part that's other-focused is enhanced, so we are more outward focused and oriented to others with empathy and compassion.

So, in summary, daily practice of relaxation or meditation strengthens the lateral prefrontal cortex, weakening the unhelpful parts of the medial prefrontal cortex – self orientation – and strengthening the helpful parts – empathy and understanding of others . . . and you get a brain with increased density in the right areas. Worth the time investment of 15 minutes a day!

Advantages of Relaxation and Meditation
- Better concentration and memory.
- Increased creativity.
- Faster problem solving.
- Deeper sleep.
- Calm attitude to people issues.
- More effective immune system.
- More creative.
- More willpower.

Exercise and Nutrition
Another great way to train the brain – that is often easily ignored or undervalued, yet can make you a lot more resilient to stress and thus boost willpower – is regular physical exercise. The benefits for work are just as plentiful as they are for you personally.

Also, what you feed your body affects how much energy the prefrontal cortex has to work with. This is why nutrition is so important. Something as simple as eating more fresh food and less processed food makes more energy available to the brain and can improve every aspect of willpower. Not only will exercise and good nutrition improve your willpower at work, but they'll make you feel better as well. Exercise in particular is known for making us happy by releasing endorphins, so why not run or exercise during lunch? You will work so much better in the afternoon.

HOW TO STICK TO YOUR
WILLPOWER CHALLENGE AT WORK

I don't. . .

A study published in the *Journal of Personality and Social Psychology* showed that there is a difference between telling yourself "I can't" and "I don't". Taking back control of the situation using the phrase "I don't" has been shown to be more effective at helping you to stick to your plan and break bad habits.

Every time you tell yourself "I can't" you're creating a feedback loop that is a reminder of your limitations. This terminology indicates that you're forcing yourself to do something you don't want to do. So, try telling yourself that you don't do that bad habit, rather than punishing yourself by saying "I can't".

Ask Questions of Yourself

A study in *Psychological Science* by Senay *et al.* in 2010 revealed that asking yourself a question helps boost motivation more than a simple self-affirmation. In other words: "Will I exercise?" works better than "I will exercise".

In the study, one group of people told themselves they would complete an anagram task. The other group asked themselves whether they would complete the task.

The results showed that those who asked themselves the question solved more anagrams than those who ordered themselves. Further experiments showed that the questioning approach helped to boost internal or "intrinsic" motivation. Psychologists have found that intrinsic motivation is the strongest type, as we discovered earlier in the book. But it is fascinating how a simple change to language like this can help boost motivation.

Professor Dolores Albarracin, one of the study's authors, said:

> "We are turning our attention to the scientific study of how language affects self-regulation. Experimental methods are allowing us to investigate people's inner speech, of both the explicit and implicit variety, and how what they say to themselves shapes the course of their behaviours.

> This study represents a basic cognitive approach to how language provides a link between thoughts and action. The reason it is so interesting is that it shows that by using language analysis, we can see that cognitive ideas are relevant to objective behaviours and that the ways people talk about their behaviour internally can predict future action."

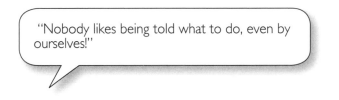

"Nobody likes being told what to do, even by ourselves!"

Well done if you have made it to the end of the book, and especially well done if during your reading you have created and pursued your own Willpower Challenge or Challenges.

Please let me know about them and I can post them on my website to encourage others to embrace willpower.

Go to www.rostaylorcompany.com/willpower.

REMINDERS

- Willpower at Work is not just about you and your willpower and ambition. It's about the business and taking others with you.
- Remember the 3 S's of Willpower at Work: Self-Awareness, Skills and Self-Preservation.
- Similar to willpower in general, you do need to establish good habits and routines at work, those of organisation, goal planning, managing distractions and completing tasks to deadlines.
- Remember to ask colleagues the three killer questions: what would they like you to stop doing, start doing, continue doing? Feedback at work is as essential as breathing.
- Rate your work culture as caring or blaming. If the latter, embark on a change programme – even if only in your own team or department.
- Remember the power of small wins.
- Use P.P.C.O. for any feedback. Talk about Plusses, Potential, Concerns and overcoming concerns.
- Mind Map – an essential for work.
- Assess your priorities at work and delegate to become successful.
- If you want to win, motivate and reward those around you.
- Increase your confidence by tackling all the questions on the Confidence Checklist.
- Love change and use the Willpower Process for Organisation Change if you want change to stick.

- Complete the Entrepreneur Quiz if you have the dream of setting up your own business. Connect with other business owners to assess what is involved. It's not for everyone.
- Look after yourself at work. Take breaks, learn to relax, sleep well and ask yourself questions instead of telling yourself what to do. We hate that!

Final Thoughts

So, to quote Eleanor Roosevelt, I hope I have given you some "willpower and skill power" to start, follow through and attain your Willpower Challenges – whatever they might be. Please share your journeys with me on our website:

www.rostaylorcompany.com/willpower

I thought for this finale I would review some highlights that I have used in my life when I required willpower. I love short memorable statements because they stick in the mind and are therefore more likely to be utilised in moments of challenge.

- **Pause and plan** This encapsulates so well the fight of your upper and lower brains, stops you in your tracks and allows a change of tactic for a new good habit to engage.
- **Mini goals** Without the small steps towards goals you have set, you are undone. They are an intrinsic part of visualising the journey. The Olympic athletes in Rio were to be seen in corners visualising their personal journeys to winning medals. We need to learn from them.
- **The 12-week rule** Three weeks for establishing a new behaviour and another nine weeks of repetition to turn that new behaviour into a habit. Never forget this one!
- **Old habits for new** Don't just stop a bad habit, replace it with something better.

Plan to fail Understand your vulnerable times and put a plan in place to cope – and for goodness sake forgive yourself for mistakes. Get back with the programme.

Willpower is a mindset The old muscle analogy doesn't reflect what we now know about willpower. Willpower is limitless, but remember: acquiring a willpower mindset is a journey not a leap.

Thoughts are not facts You can change your thinking, and if you change negatives to positives then a whole new world of possibilities opens up to you.

Externalise, externalise, externalise The toughminded phone a friend when having doubts. Anything that externalises your thinking helps – as when we become stressed our thinking and perceptions can become skewed. Become a researcher in your own thoughts. Are they correct? Change your view of yourself if not.

The 3 S's Remember Self-Awareness, Skills and Self-Preservation and act on these to become successful at work.

It's not just about you Willpower at Work requires a focus on the business and taking others with you.

Relax Almost everything is better when you are relaxed: relationships, health, creativity and, of course, willpower. Learn the skills.

Love change Take this on board personally with a growth mindset and help others at work understand the nature of willpower and its effect on change.

HIGHLIGHTS

I did finish the *Willpower* book, as you can see, and adhered to the time-table I set at the beginning. There is nothing like a deadline to keep you focused.

I did swim everyday while in Lanzarote, but returned to exercising three times a week on my return – so I really have to work on fitting in exercise on a daily basis, especially when I'm travelling. That's an ongoing Will-power Challenge for me.

Good luck and success with your Willpower Challenges.

Acknowledgements

Many thanks to my husband John Young who at times of book writing calls himself "the butler", as he has to do everything. This time he must also be thanked for his diagrammatic input.

My researcher Anna Cook Broussine was a fantastic help with interviews and data collection. Marlyn Sharpe was a godsend for re-adjusting my questionnaires.

Finally, thanks to all the wonderful people who gave of their time to be interviewed about willpower. Their courage, tenacity and insight were inspirational.

About the Author

Ros Taylor is a leading UK and international clinical psychologist, corporate and leadership coach, business woman, author, TV and radio presenter and commentator.

Featuring regularly in the national press in her capacity as a psychologist and advisor (BBC, BBC Scotland, BBC Radio 5, BBC Radio Scotland, Scottish Television, GMTV, LWT, ITN News, Sky News, Channel 4 and E4), Ros has been named by *The Independent on Sunday* as one of the top 10 coaches in Britain.

Extensive research – which included interviews with 80 of the FTSE 200's top CEOs – and her own business acumen means Ros is uniquely placed to identify areas for improvement and to implement practical and transforming solutions that really work for people and organisations.

No stranger to broadcast media, Ros was a presenter for five years on a nightly television news programme. She has written seven books, one of which provided the basis for BBC2's six-part documentary "Confidence Lab" presented by Ros. The book, *Confidence in Just Seven Days* (Vermillion 2001), topped Amazon's bestseller list. She was also the psychology consultant in the early days of "Big Brother" and "Celebrity Big Brother" on Channel 4.

Ros has written the following books:

Fast Track to the Top (Kogan Page, 2002), about success and how to achieve it.

The Ultimate Book of Confidence Tricks (Vermillion, 2003), which has been translated into nine languages.

The Complete Mind Makeover: Transform Yourself (Kogan Page, 2005).

Developing Confidence (Dorling Kindersley, 2006), part of Penguin's *Work/Life* series.

Confidence at Work (Kogan Page, 2013).

Creativity at Work (Kogan Page, 2013).

Willpower (Wiley, 2017).

Ros travels the world developing the leadership potential of employees through her Just Leadership programme. A creative academic, Ros is a chartered clinical psychologist, coach, trainer and regular speaker on the conference circuit. She has presented in the USA, Europe and China and completed a lecture tour in Japan.

In 2009, she launched Corporate Coach International, an accredited coaching school for those who want to become executive coaches.

She is a visiting professor at Strathclyde Business School, focusing on leadership, and runs her own successful leadership and coaching business: the Ros Taylor Company. She is also a non-executive director for the National Theatre for Scotland.